Falco

Jock, Paul and
swimming round the shores of
Island, off the west coast of Australia, for as long as they can remember. But suddenly their home is threatened, and their fight to save it becomes involved with the search for a sunken treasure ship in this exciting adventure story.

Joan Ambrose lives in Darlington, Western Australia. She has written many children's books, as well as plays for radio and television. *Falcon Island* is based on her script for the television series.

FALCON ISLAND

Joan Ambrose

Beaver Books

First published in 1982 by
The Hamlyn Publishing Group Limited
London · New York · Sydney · Toronto
Astronaut House, Feltham, Middlesex, England
Paperback Division: Hamlyn Paperbacks,
Banda House, Cambridge Grove,
Hammersmith, London W6 0LE
Third impression 1982

ISBN 0 600 20555 X

Printed and bound in Great Britain by
Cox & Wyman Limited, Reading
Set in Bembo

Chapter 1

Almost every afternoon, Paul, Jock and Kate came to swim at Geelup Cove. Today they had started a race at the top of the sandhills. Kate, with her blonde pigtails flying, was beating the boys. Still ahead at the high water mark, she splashed into the water, shouting gleefully.

'I'm the winner! I'm the winner!'

In a running dive Paul and Jock hit the water seconds after her, going down deep then surfacing, shaking the water out of their hair and eyes.

'I won!' said Kate.

'Only because we gave you a start,' said Paul, with a grin, teasing her.

'Rats!' said Kate and threw water at him.

'For a little kid you're getting too smart,' said Jock, pretending to grab her. 'Do you want to be ducked?'

'No!' said Kate.

'O.K. – see if you can beat us out to the reef!' said Paul.

'I'll beat you easily,' said Kate.

The reef they swam towards was partly exposed due to low tide. It was capped with small white-topped waves and fringed with seaweed, and it curved to form a natural basin, a perfect place for kids to swim. To Kate and the boys, Geelup Cove was their favourite beach by a long way.

Like most of the bays on Falcon Island, Geelup Cove was ringed with limestone crests and steep sandhills, and could only be reached by a rough pitted track. This afternoon, unknown to the kids, the dust on the road was being stirred up by an ancient truck with almost bald tyres. The truck bounced over the rocks and ploughed through the sand. The man driving had obviously driven along this track many times before. He avoided the potholes and rocks as if he knew exactly where each of them would be. Eventually he stopped at a point where the track widened.

Jack Brady got out of his truck. He was dressed in an old flannel shirt and blue serge trousers held up by fraying braces. He looked as if he were used to knocking about and living fairly rough. Now he looked around in a cautious way as if he wanted to make sure that there was nobody about. Except for the cry of a curlew the place seemed deserted. Satisfied, he went to the back of his truck and took out a shovel and a canvas bag. He hesitated for a moment, then looked inside the bag to check if the things he needed were still there. They were.

'Righto! Get going!' he said to himself. Picking up his shovel and the bag, Brady looked about again, as if to reassure himself once more that he wasn't being observed. Then he quickly headed into the scrub and with an urgent sense of purpose began to climb the nearest sandhill.

Kate, having lost the race out to the reef to Jock, had come back to the beach and was swimming lazily at the water's edge. Paul and Jock had put on their snorkels and masks and were diving on the reef where it had eroded to form hollows and shallow caves. Paul always liked to think that these hollows were deep dark caverns, but really they were just small holes in the reef. The big underwater caverns were on the dangerous western side of the island where they weren't allowed to go.

However, for Paul, Geelup Cove was fascinating. He and Jock often found all sorts of things. He had quite a collection at home – a brass compass from a Japanese fighting boat, an old sealing harpoon, part of an old lantern, and lots of sea-washed glass. Secretly, Paul was always hoping to find something else – evidence.

Evidence that would lead to locating the wreck of the old Dutch sailing ship, the *Golden Falcon*, which had disappeared in a wild July storm in the year 1647. Island legend had it that the old ship went down near Falcon Island, but the tantalising thing was that, apart from an old battered figurehead – a carved wooden falcon – that now stood in the town square, nothing else had ever been found. It was Paul's dream that one day he might be the one to find her final tragic resting-place. So each time he went swimming, Paul was hoping for some sort of clue.

Up on the sandhill, out of sight of the beach, Jack Brady was beginning to feel more than a little frustrated. He had been digging for half an hour, and he had dug at least a dozen holes in various places in the sandhills, but he still hadn't found a trace of what he was looking for. He stopped digging and wiped the sweat off his face with his sleeve. He assessed the sandhills again. Then he made a decision. He picked up his canvas bag and shovel and walked a few hundred metres. He wasn't going to give up easily. His whole future could depend on what he might find. He marked out a square and began to dig again with even more determination.

Jock had joined Kate on the beach and was helping her build a sand castle. Paul was still diving on the reef, going a little further, exploring a little more, but today he hadn't found anything. It was disappointing. He was just about to surface, to return to the beach, when he caught a glint of something on the sea floor. It was a small round object. For a minute he wasn't sure. But there it was! He dived and grabbed it. He surfaced and wrenched off his mask. Excitedly he looked at the object in his hand. It was definitely a coin! The merest glint of silver showed through the sea encrustation, but there was no mistaking it – it was a coin. He was so excited he could hardly shout.

'I've got one. I've got one!'

At the water's edge, Jock and Kate looked up. Paul was swimming towards them very fast. Jock and Kate exchanged surprised looks. For a moment Kate was concerned.

'What's the matter with Paul?'

'Maybe he's been stung by something,' Jock said.

They both stood up, waiting. But Paul, coming through the shallows, was so elated it was obvious that he wasn't hurt.

'I've got one! I've got one!'

'You scared us – we thought it was a shark or something,' said Kate.

'No – it's this!' said Paul with a flourish. He opened his clenched hand. Jock and Kate looked at him, amazed. All they could see was a flat, disc-shaped object, encrusted with coral and sea growth – nothing to get excited about.

'Is that it? It doesn't look much!' said Jock.

'But what is it?' said Kate.

'It's a Dutch guilder,' said Paul proudly.

'Oh!' said Kate.

'Are you sure?' said Jock. 'It just looks like a bit of coral to me.'

'It's been in the water for three hundred years – of course it doesn't look much!' said Paul impatiently.

Their heads were together as Paul turned the coin over and showed them the narrow rim of silver under the sea encrustation.

'See!' The sun caught the flash of silver.

'Wow! If it's a guilder I suppose it's worth a fair bit,' said Jock.

'Hundreds of dollars,' said Paul.

'Fantastic!' said Jock, now much more impressed.

Paul was trying to scrape off some of the encrustation with his fingernail to reveal more of the coin, but the coral-like growth was so hard that he couldn't make any impression on it.

After her initial enthusiasm, Kate suddenly became doubtful.

'Are you sure it's a guilder, Paul?'

'Of course I am!' said Paul, scornfully.

'But everybody reckons the *Golden Falcon* would have been wrecked on the other side of the island – not here.'

'How would you know?' said Paul, not prepared to accept any doubts.

'Dad says.'

'I've never heard Dad say that,' Paul's reaction was sharp.

Kate bit her lip. Paul looked at her as if she were trying to spoil something – she didn't want to do that. They had always been told that the ocean currents and the old records in the museum could only mean one thing – the wreck was probably on the western side of the island – if it existed at all. And lots of people thought that it didn't.

'I just wondered,' said Kate.

Paul's excitement had faded a little.

'Well, I think it's a guilder,' he said, and he put it very carefully in the zip pocket of his swimming shorts. The way he did it indicated that he wasn't going to talk about it any more. Then he picked up his towel.

'Let's go. It's time we were getting home.'

'Paul!' said Kate. But Paul was already walking ahead of them very fast.

Jock pulled a face. 'Now you've done it!' he said to Kate, ruefully.

Kate trailed behind the boys. The afternoon was really spoilt. It didn't matter any more that the sun was still warm and the bay sheltered and peaceful, with the seagulls gliding over the sun-tipped water, searching for their evening meal. But all the same, Kate thought, Paul had no right to get angry just because she had pointed out something that was true. And Miss Fitzgerald had taught them about it at school as well. All about the skill of the Dutch seamen, and their ships laden with goods from Amsterdam – crockery, tools, flagons of Rhenish wine, and the latest fashions in silk and velvet – and how powerless were the strongest ships and the bravest sailors when they met the fury of the westerly winter storms.

Ahead of Kate, Paul had recovered some of his excitement.

'As soon as I get home', he said to Jock, 'I'm going to show this to Dad. He'll know whether it's a guilder or not.'

'What about Mrs Yates at the Post Office? She's interested in the history of the island . . . she'd probably know. . . .' But then Jock suddenly stopped, looking over the top of the sandhill. A wary and puzzled expression had come over his face. Paul was surprised at the abrupt way Jock had stopped speaking, but then he too saw what had caught Jock's attention, and was suddenly a bit scared. Less than a hundred metres away was their old enemy, Jack Brady. Cantankerous, grumpy Jack Brady who didn't like kids. He was digging – and somehow it didn't look right.

Kate, from below, suddenly saw the boys flatten to the ground. Then Paul quickly looked around to see where she was. He gave her a warning gesture that she was to come up the track quietly.

Jock was staring at Brady. The hole was long, narrow and deep.

'What is it, d'you reckon?' he whispered.

'Don't know,' Paul whispered back. Kate flung herself beside them.

'Crikey!' she said, looking at Brady, labouring, hot and sweaty. 'What's he doing?'

'Don't know,' said Paul. He was puzzled. Why should Brady be digging a trench? And all the other holes nearby, what were they?

'Perhaps it's for bait,' said Kate.

'Not up here in this dry sand,' said Jock.

'Then what?'

Something, some flurry of movement or some natural sense of caution, suddenly made Brady stop digging. His eyes narrowed. Squinting into the sun he became aware of three heads – two blonde and a darker one. The Ellery kids and that Dixon kid! For a moment he almost panicked. He'd thought the place was deserted. And now here were these kids – you couldn't move on this island without tripping over confounded kids! He certainly wasn't going to have them hanging around. Not now. Brady took a step forward. 'You!' he shouted. 'Go on – clear off!'

'Wow! – He's really bad-tempered today,' said Kate, scared, ducking out of sight.

Jock, however, was prepared to defy Brady. They weren't doing any harm. He glanced at Paul for encouragement. Paul nodded. Jock called back:

'We've just been swimming, Mr Brady.'

His tone was just a shade too innocent, it bordered on cheek, and Brady wasn't having any of it. He proceeded towards them a little further, carrying his shovel. His manner was menacing.

'I told you – buzz off! Go on, buzz off!'

Kate, stirred by Jock's defiance, muttered under her breath, 'Buzz off yourself, you old stinker!'

It was impossible, but it seemed that Brady had heard her. He continued walking up the hill, waving his shovel, and shouting,

'Go on – you kids clear out! You're on private property. You've no business being here.'

'Wow! – let's get out of here,' said Paul. It really looked as if Brady meant what he said. 'If he tells Dad we'll get into trouble. We're not supposed to go on anyone's property.'

'Yeah! Let's go!' said Jock.

Kate and the boys took off, running fast over the hill and down through the scrub. They kept going until they reached their bikes, puffing and panting, from running through the soft sand. Then they stopped. Sweat was making Paul's hair cling to his forehead, Kate had a stitch, and Jock was out of breath.

'Well, what set him off?' said Jock, when he'd recovered a little.

'It's obvious he didn't want us hanging around,' said Paul.

'I wonder why not,' said Jock.

Kate had an idea.

'I bet he's digging a grave!'

Jock had thought this himself when they'd first seen the hole Brady was digging. It looked like a grave, but if he had something to bury, like a dead fowl or something, why come all the way out to Geelup Cove? It didn't make sense. Now Jock felt he could be a bit superior about it.

'Of course he isn't,' he said.

'Well, it looked like a grave to me.'

'Don't be dopey, Kate. Where's the body? The head? In his old canvas bag?'

'All right, clever!' said Kate. 'You tell me. Why did he chase us away?'

Jock, however, was really taken with the idea of Brady burying a body, and he thought the way they had been so scared of Brady was really funny. After all, he was only old Brady. Jock pretended he was throwing the legs of a corpse into the hole Brady had dug.

'Brady throws in the legs,' he said. 'Oh blast! – they're too big!'

With a theatrical gesture, he pretended that he had to break the legs in half.

'. . . And now the arms, and the knobbly bits – ribs and that!'

'. . . And blood!' said Paul, gorily.

'Yeah – it's all dripping with blood,' said Jock with relish.

Kate had covered her face.

'Yuk! Don't! You make me feel sick.' And she did look a bit squeamish and green.

Paul realised that Kate was upset. After all, she was

only eight. He put an arm around her to comfort her.

'It's only a game,' he said. The sun was starting to go down behind the hills and trees. 'Anyway, we'd better go home. We have to get things from the shop.'

They got on their bikes and started to ride home through the scrub and the she-oak grove. Jock and Kate rode ahead. Paul, behind them, was in a thoughtful mood. He was thinking of the coin in his pocket, his guilder. And he was thinking about Brady. Why had Brady chased them away? He was a bad-tempered old thing, but he'd never been so aggressive before. What secret did he have?

Soon they were at the outskirts of the town, and riding past the small weatherboard houses with their neat gardens. Almost every house had a small boat or fishing nets and cray pots in the yard, indicating the closeness of the islanders to the sea. Despite their tidiness, most of the houses needed painting and had an air of poverty about them.

As the kids reached the town square, they saw that the Post Office Store was still open. They would be in time to get the bread. Paul was still very preoccupied. In the town square, near the Post Office, was the familiar battered monument, the figurehead from the *Golden Falcon*. As they rode past it, Paul suddenly wheeled and stopped. He was gripped with incredible excitement as he looked up at the beady wooden eye of the carved falcon which stared down at him, imperturbable and secretive.

'Paul!' called Kate.

But Paul didn't hear her.

'Now what?' said Jock. Jock and Kate walked back to Paul, still near the falcon.

'Paul!' said Kate, beside him. 'Do we have to get milk as well as bread tonight?'

But Paul seemed to be almost in a trance.

'Paul!' said Kate again, impatiently.

Paul turned to Kate and Jock.

'I know what old Brady's doing – he's not digging a grave! I bet he's found relics from the *Golden Falcon*!'

'Yeah?' Jock and Kate were incredulous.

Paul's whole face was alight.

'Yeah – that's what he's doing. He's found relics. They could be worth thousands and thousands of dollars.'

'Wow!' said Kate.

'Well, I expect you might be right,' said Jock slowly.

'Might be right?' insisted Paul. 'Of course I'm right!'

It seemed so obvious to Paul – high in the sand dunes Brady had found evidence of the *Golden Falcon* and valuable objects as well. That was why he had chased them away. He didn't want anybody to know – he wanted everything for himself.

'I don't see how the *Golden Falcon* could have got so far up on the beach,' said Jock.

'Not the *Golden Falcon,* dope! The sailors. I reckon some sailors got ashore and camped there.'

'I suppose there could have been some survivors,' said Jock, but he didn't sound very convinced.

Mrs Yates, a motherly figure, looked out from the Post Office Store and saw Jock, Kate and Paul standing beside the monument. Mrs Yates had a soft spot for children, especially Kate and Paul. She got their bread, wrapped it up, and put it on the counter with their milk order, ready for them. She expected they would arrive in a moment or two.

Paul was still trying to persuade Jock.

'Look – if he'd found silver guilders . . . like this,' Paul took out his coin, '– don't you see – he wouldn't want anybody to know!'

'Yeah – I suppose,' said Jock. 'Yeah – I suppose you're right.'

'And that's what that bag was for!'

'Yeah!' Jock whistled. His face broke into a broad grin. 'Aren't things like that supposed to go to museums?'

'That's right,' said Kate.

'Trust old Brady!' said Jock. 'He'd nick anything.'

'Hey – look who's coming!' said Kate in a warning tone. The boys looked back up the road. There was Brady, driving towards the town square very fast.

'Gee! He's in a hurry!' exclaimed Jock.

Brady swung sharply into the town square and pulled up in the parking area near the hotel.

As if of one accord, the kids had made a decision and ducked out of sight behind the monument. Then they cautiously crept around to watch him, ready to note anything that might confirm their suspicions. But all Brady did was to head for the phone box. That didn't tell them anything. There was nothing unusual in that. But to Paul, somehow, Brady seemed very pleased with himself. Or was he imagining it?

It was Jock who saw the canvas bag on the back of Brady's truck.

'Hey!' he said, nudging Paul. 'Look – there's that canvas bag Brady had with him when he was digging. I wonder if there are some things in it? I wouldn't mind having a look.'

Jock was ready to dare. Paul hesitated a little.

'Come on!' said Jock.

Kate took fright. 'You can't!'

Jock shot a look at Brady, now involved in a telephone conversation, huddled, with his back turned as if he didn't want to be overheard. 'It's O.K.,' he said.

'I'm not going to be in it,' said Kate. 'I'm getting the bread.'

She didn't want to be caught. She ran off to the store as fast as she could.

The boys began approaching Brady's truck, sizing up how they could get a quick look inside the canvas bag without anyone noticing. Paul, heart beating a little fast, wished he had Jock's confidence. Jock was calmly sauntering across the town square, whistling, hands in his pockets – very cool indeed, but completely out of character. Paul tried to do the same. If Brady had seen them he would have realised that they were up to something straight away. They were about as inconspicuous as if they'd decided to cross the town square in Samurai wigs.

But they were lucky. Kate, now dashing out of the Store with an ice cream from Mrs Yates, and the bread and milk, collided with Brady the very second he left the phone box. Head down, she butted him right in the stomach. Brady gasped. For a moment all he could do was stand there, eyes popping, winded.

'Ooeewh!' he wheezed, like a slowly deflating balloon. Frightened, Kate dropped the bread but managed to hang on to the milk and her ice cream.

She looked up, her big blue eyes wide, terrified. Then the inevitable happened. Her ice cream dropped. It dropped unerringly on to the top of Brady's boot. Slowly some of it melted and trickled down his sock. Brady looked at it in disbelief. However, the soggy cold seemed to revive him.

'Hey!' he growled. 'Watch where you go, girlie!'

'I'm very sorry,' said Kate, almost in tears.

'Damn!' said Brady, as the ice cream melted further.

Kate took the chance and fled.

As they rode home, Kate was furious with the boys. They couldn't stop laughing.

'He could have done anything to me,' she said indignantly. And she was also wild about losing her ice cream. The boys just kept on laughing.

'You were safe,' they said. 'You nearly laid him out cold.'

'I saved you, anyway!' said Kate, with emphasis.

That seemed to quieten them down a bit. Then Jock said, 'I'd still like to know what he's got in that canvas bag – whether he's got any guilders.'

They were now getting very close to where Kate

and Paul lived. Their street branched off the main road.

'Do you know what?' Jock said suddenly to Paul.

'What?'

'I reckon I'm going to have another try to see what's in that bag!'

'Yeah?' said Paul.

'Tonight,' Jock said. 'Late – after he's gone to bed!'

'What?' said Paul, quite startled.

'Yeah! Do you want to come, or are you chicken?'

Paul was a little uncertain. But he could see that Jock had his reckless look, and he was testing Paul too.

'All right. I'm not chicken,' Paul said.

They looked at Kate.

'I'm not chicken either,' said Kate boldly.

'Right,' Jock said.

Underneath, Kate was feeling trembly – in fact she didn't feel very bold at all.

'Wear something dark,' Jock said as he was about to ride off.

'Why? What for?' asked Kate.

Jock sighed, as if she were really stupid.

'Camouflage – like the commandos,' he said.

Kate felt even less confident. What did Jock intend to do? She didn't like to ask.

Chapter 2

That evening, although both Kate and Paul were wondering what they had committed themselves to, the Ellery household seemed much the same as on any other day.

'Now, let's have another look at this guilder of yours,' said Frank, their father, as they were finishing tea. Paul fished in his pocket and found his guilder. Frank examined the sea-encrusted coin with great interest.

'It's certainly been in the water a long time,' said Frank.

'Do you think it could be a guilder?' asked Paul.

'You'd have to ask an expert,' said Frank. 'But it's a possibility, I suppose.' He handed the coin back to Paul, knowing how much Paul would treasure it. He was very aware of his son's great interest in the old Dutch wreck.

'What's for pudding?' asked Kate.

'Rock melon,' said Frank, getting it from the old fridge. 'And what did you do today, Katey?'

'Well,' Kate began, as if she were about to launch into the whole story. Paul kicked her under the table.

'Oh – er, nothing much,' she said quickly, taking the hint, and wishing Paul didn't kick so hard. 'Oh yeah – Mrs Yates gave me an ice cream.'

'She shouldn't. She spoils you,' Frank said.

'She's always spoiling us,' said Kate. 'But I think she likes you best, Dad.'

Frank laughed, eyes twinkling. Ever since their mother had died the kids had been on the look out for any prospective stepmother.

'You've got the wrong idea about Dorothy Yates,' said Frank. 'She's a bit old for me, anyway.'

'That doesn't stop them,' said Kate. '. . . Mrs Mortimer is really old, and she likes you too.'

It was true. His warmth and good nature made Frank popular with everyone on Falcon Island.

'Don't worry,' said Frank. 'I like things the way they are.'

That pleased the kids.

Frank then went to watch the news on television, looking forward to relaxing after a busy day. His job with the Council included being a wildlife Ranger, and today he and Alf Dixon, Jock's grandfather, had been cutting firebreaks through the Reserve – hard, heavy work. Kate and Paul washed up and stacked the dishes on the dresser.

From then on the evening seemed endless. The old clock on the mantelpiece ticked so slowly. Paul wished that he hadn't agreed to Jock's plan to go to Brady's house. He wished that he could call it off, but he couldn't be chicken. Eventually it was time to go to bed. Kate was already asleep as Paul quietly wound up his alarm clock, setting it for eleven o'clock. He put it under his pillow and lay back, letting his mind drift over all that had happened that day.

Paul was dreaming about his guilder when the alarm went off in his ear. He turned it off and was out of bed in an instant, shaking Kate. They dressed quickly and, carrying their gym shoes, crept out of the house. The lights were still on in the living room. Their father had fallen asleep in front of the television set. But he didn't stir. Their hearts beating fast, they reached the front gate. It squeaked. They froze and waited, listening. Nothing happened. Without wasting any time, Paul and Kate ran past the illuminating glare of the street light, up the road and into the bush. Picking up the track, they tried not to notice how different the moon made the familiar trees and bushes. To Kate it seemed that some of the trees looked like evil, crouching demons, and their leaves shadowy, clutching fingers.

Finally they reached the meeting place. Jock emerged from the shadows. He had taken the dark bit seriously. He wore black corduroy pants and a black T-shirt and had painted his face black as well.

'Gee, you look awful!' said Kate.

It made the whites of his eyes stand out like frog's eyes.

'It's only Nan's stove black,' said Jock.

'Will it come off?'

Jock apparently hadn't thought of that.

'Crumbs! Hope so.' However, worrying about getting clean again wasn't his first priority. There were other things to do.

'O.K.,' said Jock. 'Let's get a look at that canvas bag.' He led the way through the dark. Paul was a little envious. Jock didn't seem in the least bit nervous, whereas he was feeling dry-mouthed and uneasy, and Kate seemed to be too, by the way she gripped his hand.

Brady's house was at the end of the township. It was a tumbledown weatherboard building with lots of junk, old fishing nets, craypots, bits of old trucks and petrol drums scattered around the yard, all of which Brady had some plan for some time in the future when he got round to it.

Thankfully the front of the house was in darkness and there was no street light. Jock opened the front gate, then he beckoned Paul and Kate to follow. They tiptoed on to the front verandah. The floor creaked then groaned.

'What was that?' Kate whispered, petrified.

'Nothing,' whispered Jock, moving forward stealthily. To Kate it was unbelievable that Jock should be so calm. Her heart was thumping so loudly she thought that Brady must surely hear it.

They crept further along the verandah. There was a narrow crack between the blind and the window of the front room. They peered in cautiously. The light was on, but apart from the fact that Brady's living room was as untidy as his back yard, there was no sign of him, and no sign of the canvas bag.

'He hasn't gone to bed,' said Paul. 'What do we do?'

'We'll go round the back,' whispered Jock.

He stepped off the front verandah on to a path that led to the back of Brady's house. The side of the house, shadowed by trees, was in greater darkness. Jock now moved forward with confidence. In the dark he failed to see an old axle hidden in the grass. He collided with it and pitched forward. He fell against a lopsided stack of bottles heaped against the house.

'Blast!' said Jock, forgetting to be quiet, as he rubbed his sore shin.

'Ssh! Keep quiet!' whispered Paul urgently. However, Paul's warning was lost in the sound: A bottle had slipped. Then another. Then the whole stack began to slide. It gained momentum. The kids looked at it in horror, the whites of Jock's eyes in his blackened face standing out goggle-eyed. Then there was an almighty crash. A bottle smashed. Then another. To the kids the sound seemed as loud as cannon fire. And it seemed to reverberate on and on and on.

'Idiot!' hissed Paul, terrified, sure that Brady would come roaring out and find them at any minute. 'Why didn't you look where you were going?'

'Didn't see them in the dark,' said Jock, his hands clammy. Another bottle moved. They waited for the crash. They waited but it didn't come. Then Jock saw the funny side.

'Ten green bottles . . .' he began to sing, '. . . at Brady's house they fell,' he giggled. It didn't rhyme very well. 'And one green bottle accidentally . . .' he went on.

Paul grabbed him and shook him.

'Shut up!'

'Let's go home,' said Kate, almost in tears.

'Don't lose your sense of perspective,' Jock said haughtily. Paul had no sense of humour.

Paul ignored him. He was listening again. There were no footsteps, no shouts. It seemed that old Brady hadn't heard, or if he had, he'd put the noise down to stray cats prowling in the yard.

Paul now began to feel a little reassured. A light shone from the back of the house. It seemed worth investigating further.

'Let's try the kitchen,' he said.

'No. Let's go,' said Kate, wishing she were safe at home in bed.

Paul grabbed her hand to give her greater confidence and, creeping carefully past the stack of bottles, led her and Jock towards Brady's kitchen window.

The kitchen window was wide open and the light dazzlingly bright. They paused, hidden well back in the shadows. Their eyes took a moment to adjust to the light. Brady was nowhere about.

'A bit closer,' said Paul.

They crept up and looked in. They were right. The room was empty. And there on the kitchen table under the window was what they had come to find – the canvas bag!

'I can get it,' said Jock

Suddenly there was an ear-splitting, blood-curdling screech. Their hearts nearly stopped. They dropped down. Paul felt a cold sweat on the back of his neck, and Jock beside him was trembling. Kate was huddled, frozen, hands over her eyes. What was it? Then it happened again. It sounded like the death-rattle of a vampire. But then Paul thought there was something strangely familiar about it – the words. The screech came again.

'Miserable old coot!' it screamed. Then a pause. Then the voice changed and it began to sing in a scratchy, off-key way. Paul lifted his head. He looked in the window.

'Dance cocky, dance cocky. Give us a kiss, give us a kiss.' It was Brady's old bald-headed pink cockatoo in his cage in the corner of the room, dancing up and down on his perch, with an empty seed dish in one claw. Paul felt an enormous sense of relief. He thought the sound must have been made by a blood-sucking bat at least.

Jock and Kate had seen him too.

'Well, what do you know!' said Jock in disgust. 'It's Brady's cockatoo!' His sense of pride had been hurt. Being made a fool of by an old cockatoo! The bag was still there on the kitchen table, tantalisingly close.

'I can get that bag,' Jock said to Paul. He was determined to.

'Give me a leg-up.'

Paul sized up the distance. The bag was very close.

'Right,' he said.

Jock put his foot into Paul's cupped hand. Paul gave Jock a lift. Jock pulled himself up on to the windowsill. He leant forward. His hand reached out. Then a door on the opposite side of the room began to open. Brady! Jock dropped to the ground just in time. Brady entered the kitchen.

'What are you making a row for, you silly old devil?' Brady said. He saw the empty seed dish, put down the things he was carrying and filled it.

'That'll do you,' he said, and threw a cover over the cage.

'It's hopeless,' whispered Paul. 'Let's go home.'

Kate nodded. But Jock held Paul's arm. He had seen something he wanted to verify. Slowly he peeped over the windowsill. He motioned Paul to do the same. What they saw was amazing. Brady had put a pair of shoes and a tin of shoe polish on the kitchen table. And now he was holding up a suit, which he was brushing down with a clothes brush. Jock and Paul looked at one another in astonishment. What did this mean? Brady always wore working clothes – old trousers, a flannel shirt and working boots. He never wore good clothes.

Kate now decided that she had enough courage to take a quick look as well. Brady was still brushing his suit. One glance was enough. Kate knew.

'Brady's going to the mainland tomorrow!' she said. 'I bet he's going to sell those things from the *Golden Falcon*.'

Jock and Paul were still discussing Brady when they reached the shadowy fork in the road where they would have to separate to go home.

'I reckon we should have waited and got the bag after he went to bed,' argued Jock yet again.

'Use your head,' said Paul. 'What would you have done about the bird? Choked it or wrung its neck or what?'

'You give up too easily,' said Jock. 'Anyway, he wouldn't have seen us with the cover over his cage.'

'Rubbish! He'd have heard us!'

Kate had had enough. The boys had been wrangling like this all the way home. The moon was now passing through cloud, and she was almost asleep on her feet. All she wanted to do was to go home and go to bed.

'Come on, Paulie. Let's go.'

The plaintive exhausted note in her voice made Paul realise guiltily that it was very, very late.

'All right,' he said.

Jock was still full of fight. After all this he didn't want to concede victory to Brady.

'We can't let Brady get away with it just like that!'

'What else can we do?' Paul wanted to forget the whole matter and go.

Jock thought, then his face lit up.

'We'll get up early. We'll come back.'

'Oh no!' Kate groaned.

However, Paul agreed at once.

'Right! Early.'

'O.K.,' said Jock. 'See you.' He disappeared quickly in the darkness with a cheerful, jaunty whistle.

'We'll soon be home,' Paul said to Kate. They half walked, half ran home. The house was in darkness. They crept in. In bed Kate fell asleep at once.

Sleep came more slowly for Paul. The excitement of the night's events remained with him. He could hear the booming of the surf on the beach. His thoughts went back to his guilder, and the deep, blue-green secret hollows of the reef at Geelup Cove. Then he began to drift off, and before long he too was asleep.

The family arrangements were that Paul and Kate would get their own breakfast and tidy the house every morning as Frank Ellery left for work before seven. The next morning, despite the fact that they were tired and Kate kept stifling a yawn, they did their jobs in record time. They were out of the door, on to their bikes and riding up the road to meet Jock while it was still quite early and most of the houses on Falcon Island had a half-asleep look.

Jock was waiting for them at the fork in the road. Kate noticed a rim of black around the edge of his face, a tidemark around his ears and down his neck.

'You didn't get all the black off,' she said.

Jock gave her a withering look. There were times when Kate got stuck on irrelevancies, and this was one of them.

'Never mind that,' he said. 'Let's get there.'

They rode quickly towards Brady's house. There was no cover of darkness now, so they dumped their bikes in bushes and then began a cautious approach for the last twenty metres, keeping hidden in the scrub.

They'd reached a thick broom bush. The front of Brady's house could be seen clearly.

'His truck's still there,' Paul whispered.

He was about to creep forward when he stopped abruptly. Brady had come out of the house. He was carrying the canvas bag, and looking quite unlike himself in his blue suit and tie and dark felt hat. He was obviously going to the mainland. Paul felt a rush of excitement. Then Brady put the canvas bag in the back of the truck.

Alarmed, Jock whispered. 'We're too late! He's going. Think of something to divert him. Quick!'

'What do you want me to do? Go and ask Brady the time or something?'

'No, stupid!' Jock hissed, then added, 'Just a minute!' They watched as Brady looked inside the truck as if searching for something. Then he felt in his pockets. The kids were close enough to see that he had a puzzled frown on his face. Then, with a gesture of irritation, he went back to the house, still patting his pockets as if searching for something he had mislaid.

'Right! Now!' urged Paul.

Kate, Paul and Jock darted from where they were hidden, almost tripping over one another in nervous haste. Brady had thrown the canvas bag into the back of the truck in such a way that it was almost impossible for them to get at it and to remain on the far side, out of sight and within the reach of concealing shrubs. Jock was determined, however. He tried to climb over the side of the truck, but it was difficult. He was in danger of being stuck half way. And then how would he explain what he was doing? He was so anxious to grab the bag and to prevent Brady from taking the things that he had found from the *Golden Falcon* that he was prepared to risk anything.

'Hang on to me,' he said to Paul. Paul hung on to Jock's legs as he tried to grab the elusive bag, which was just a fingertip out of reach.

'I'll get it,' said Kate, wanting to help.
'No,' said Jock. 'I've nearly got it.'
He leant forward. Just another centimetre, half a centimetre, and he'd be able to get it. But at the very second that he almost had the strap in his hand, Brady came out of his back door, shutting it with a bang.
'Drop!' said Paul. Jock dropped. There was nothing else he could do but to wriggle in beside Paul in the bushes and to hide as Brady hurried towards his truck. Brady didn't look around. He got into the truck, started the motor, slammed it into gear and accelerated down the drive.
In the hedge Jock was coping with his disappointment. He'd nearly had the bag. Another ten seconds and he would have succeeded. He was so disappointed that for a moment he didn't notice that Kate wasn't with them.
'Hey! Where's Kate?' he began. But then he could tell by the look on Paul's face that Paul was numb with shock.
'What's the matter?'
'She – she climbed in over the back of Brady's truck!' Paul managed to say. 'Just as you jumped down!'
'Christopher!' said Jock. 'Come on!'
Paul and Jock raced down Brady's drive, expecting to see Kate's body lying on the road. But the road was empty. There was nothing there. All they could see was the rear lights of his truck and a cloud of dust as Brady braked fast at the corner. He was heading in the direction of the jetty.
'The bikes!' shouted Paul.
The boys rushed to their bikes and were soon following down the road, as fast as they had ever ridden, each one terrified of what might happen to Kate if she fell out, and also what might happen to her if Brady found her.
But Kate, after her initial shock of being jolted flat in the back of the truck when Brady took off so abruptly, had decided that the safest thing to do was to stay lying

flat and to hope that she wouldn't bounce out of the open end. It was very difficult to cling to the sides. Brady seemed to be driving over every rut and pothole in the road. But she hung on. She didn't have time to think of any consequences if Brady found her. She was concentrating on not ending up on the road.

The boys rode as fast as they could but Brady lost them. But at least it seemed that Kate hadn't fallen out. She wasn't on the road. Out of breath and panting they rounded a corner two hundred metres from the jetty car park. Brady was just pulling up. They saw him get out of his truck. He went round the back. They could hardly bear to look. Then they couldn't believe their eyes. He leant in, picked up his canvas bag, then without stopping and in a very businesslike way he hurried off towards the jetty where his boat was moored.

'Where's Kate?' said Paul, completely white.

Jock scarcely knew how to reply. Kate must have fallen off somewhere.

'Brady wasn't going that fast,' he said. But even to himself his voice didn't sound very convincing.

Paul got on his bike to ride back to find her, not daring to think how badly she might be hurt or what might have happened. He felt sick in the pit of his stomach. His sense of anxiety was so great that he didn't see a small blonde head poke out of the roadside scrub a short distance further along the road near the car park. Kate could see that Brady was already on the jetty and about to get into his boat, so she knew she was safe. She put her fingers in her mouth and gave a piercing whistle. Paul nearly fell off his bike in shock.

'There she is!' shouted Jock.

The boys sprinted up the road.

'What happened?' said Paul, when they reached her.

'Did you fall off? Are you all right?'

'Of course I'm all right,' said Kate, feeling pleased with herself. 'When he started to slow down I slid out the back and got into the bush and ran off fast.' She giggled. 'Brady never knew I was there.' She'd managed to fool old Brady. That idea really appealed to her.

Paul was still concerned. 'Are you sure you haven't hurt yourself?' he said.

'No! I'm all right,' Kate said. Then she added, 'Don't you want to see what I got?'

The boys' reaction was instantaneous and incredulous.

'What did you get? What is it?'

'Did you get something?'

'You bet,' said Kate, fishing in her shirt. 'I didn't get on Brady's truck just for the ride.'

For once the boys allowed this small kid smart-talk to pass. They were too anxious to see what she had.

'Show us!' said Paul.

Kate handed Paul a small plastic bag – a freezer bag. It had a number scrawled on it in felt-tip pen, and the top was secured with a twist-around tag. Paul had trouble undoing the tag. He couldn't get it off. He didn't want to rip it.

Jock and Kate were impatient.

'Come on! Let's see!'

'I'm doing my best,' said Paul. In his haste he was all fingers and thumbs. At last he got the tag off and opened the bag. He tipped out some of the contents. The kids were absolutely stunned.

'Sand!' exclaimed Kate.

'It's just a bag of black sand,' said Paul in bewilderment as he tipped out a little more.

'Are you sure that's all there was? There weren't any coins, or something like that?'

Kate was completely deflated. Her moment of triumph had gone quite flat.

'No,' she replied, upset. 'Just lots of bags like that.'

'There must have been something else,' Jock insisted. 'Were they all the same?'

'Yes, I just told you,' said Kate crossly, but also close

to tears. She felt so stupid. All of that for bags of sand!

Jock and Paul were totally perplexed.

'Do you reckon old Brady's gone off his nut or something?' Jock said.

Paul, still bewildered, was now squatting on the road. He had pulled out his handkerchief and was pouring the sand slowly into it. Jock and Kate squatted down beside him. He carefully spread the sand out. The plastic bag contained absolutely nothing except black sand and a few knobbly bits of stone.

'Brady's got to be off his head,' said Jock. 'Packing up bags of sand and taking them to the mainland! It's crazy.'

'Yes,' said Kate. 'He must be nuts.'

Paul, however, was intrigued by several oddly shaped objects in the sand.

'Look at this!' he said, his excitement rising. 'This is a bone. I'm sure it's a bone. Could be part of a skeleton.'

'What did I tell you?' said Kate. 'I said he was burying a body!'

'The skeleton of a Dutch sailor, I mean, dope!' said Paul.

Jock was sceptical.

'It looks like a bit of limestone to me.'

At that moment the familiar and insistent sound of the school bell reached them from across the town.

'Quick!' said Kate. 'We'd better go, or Miss Fitzgerald will be mad.'

Kate's bike was way back near Brady's house. There wasn't time to go back and get it now.

'I'll carry you on my crossbar,' said Jock.

Kate got on to Jock's bike and he began to ride back up the road as the school bell rang again. Behind them Paul was carefully tipping the black sand back into the plastic bag and securing it again with the tag. Thoughtfully Paul picked up his bike. The whole thing intrigued him. Riding slowly he considered everything that had happened.

Had Brady found part of a skeleton? Then the school bell began ringing again with even more insistence and he had to ride fast to get to school before everyone else went in. He just made it, running up the steps in time to see Miss Fitzgerald raise her eyebrows at the tidemark around Jock's neck.

'In a rush this morning?' she said to Jock.

'Yes, Miss,' said Jock. Miss Fitzgerald patted him on the shoulder and laughed.

'Thought so,' she said. 'Remind me to have a hygiene lesson about soap and water later on!'

Chapter 3

In school that morning, Paul found he couldn't concentrate. His mind kept wandering to the puzzle of Brady and all the things that had happened. From his desk he could look right out of the window, across the lawn, through the drooping peppermint trees to the bay. The sea in the sunlight was a magnificent blue, reflecting the infinity of the blue of the sky, and the small boats tied up at the jetty seemed almost unreal, like toys. There was the familiar line of boats: Alan's, Jock's, Grandpop's small dinghy the *Urchin*, *Fly Away* which belonged to Harry at the pub, and several others. The only one missing was Brady's. Beyond the jetty, because there was no haze today, it was possible to pick up the gentle creaming of the waves on the reef, and beyond that a smudge of distant shoreline and buildings – the mainland.

Brady had gone to the mainland. Why? Paul scanned the bay again for any sign of Brady's boat. When would he return? He took the guilder from his pocket and examined it carefully. He was sure it must be a guilder, and he was tantalised by the thought that Brady's mysterious digging was somehow connected with his discovery of the coin in Geelup Cove.

All day Paul found that Brady's behaviour kept nagging at him. So much so that Miss Fitzgerald had to speak to him twice for inattention. It was when they were doing social studies that a further thought came into his head. Miss Fitzgerald was teaching them about air currents, so there wasn't any obvious connection between the lesson and Paul's sudden realisation that there was a factor he hadn't considered. Of course, if the sailors came ashore in Geelup Cove, it was logical that the *Golden Falcon* would have been wrecked nearby. The reef! Of course! The answer could be in the reef. His mind began to fill with plans. The thing they must do was to explore the reef in Geelup Cove. He could see himself and Jock diving and searching, uncovering the wooden ribs of the hull, cannon and gun mountings, and there would be more guilders, and sea-encrusted chests, with who knows what inside them. Gold and jewels perhaps.

In the end Paul had convinced himself so thoroughly that all they had to do was to look and they would find the wreck, that he was out of the classroom as soon as school was dismissed that afternoon, and waiting at his bike for Jock and Kate before most of the other kids had left their desks.

'Quick – we've got things to do,' he said as they strolled up to meet him.

'What's biting you?' said Jock.

'We're going to take the *Urchin* out to the reef.'

'Yeah? What for? I thought we'd go for a swim.'

'No,' said Paul.

'I'll have to get my bike and have something to eat first.' Kate wasn't going to miss out on her after-school snack.

'You can.' Paul was impatient with them both.

'Why do you want to go to the reef?'

'Well . . .' began Paul. As he rode along with Kate on the crossbar of his bike he explained his theories.

'Brady found bones. But I found a guilder. Where there's one guilder there'll be more. Out on the reef!'

'Ah! I see!' said Jock.

'We've gotta get some maps and we're going to take the *Urchin* and go out and start searching in a proper systematic way.'

'Yeah. A good idea,' said Jock. They were allowed to use the *Urchin*, his grandfather's boat, sometimes.

'You could be right.' Right or not Jock thought it would be fun. He liked diving.

'As long as I have something to eat first,' said Kate.

They got Kate's bike and it was arranged that they would meet at the jetty.

Paul and Kate rode home as fast as they could. Paul quicky rummaged through drawers and in the storage cupboard looking for old maps of the island that he remembered his father had. He was sure that there were several maps that showed the reefs and the depth of the ocean floor around the island. However, all he managed to dig out were a couple of old tourist maps that didn't have much detail. He was disappointed but they would have to do. In the meantime Kate had cut several large pieces of cake, given Paul one, and had two herself. Having satisfied her ravenous hunger, she found the life jackets which they had to wear whenever they went out in the *Urchin*. It was one of Frank Ellery's strictest rules.

Before long they were out of the house again and riding down the road. They ran clattering over the uneven wooden planks of the old jetty, pausing only to wave to Herb scaling herring on the beach. Herb gave them a friendly wave back. They liked Herb. He often gave them advice about where the fish were biting and where to net for crabs, but there was no time to stop to talk to him today.

Jock was at the end of the jetty with his snorkel and diving mask in his hand. In two seconds they were in the *Urchin*, a rough little aluminium dinghy. Kate was in the middle, Jock at the tiller. Paul unhitched the mooring line from the jetty.

'O.K., Skipper. Let's go.'

Jock pulled the starter cord. The outboard motor fired at once. Then, with a flurry of wake, they set out from the jetty heading into the sun, making their way around the promontory and Wireless Hill, into Geelup Cove. The *Urchin* bounced over the slight swell that had developed with the afternoon breeze. The wind was in Kate's face. The seagulls wheeled overhead, calling with their high-pitched mewing. There was the smell and tang of salt and seaspray. It was marvellous.

It took them only about twenty minutes to get to Geelup Cove. Jock slowed the *Urchin*. Paul had a map open on his knees. He was trying to calculate some approximate distances. He was squinting, lining up where they had seen Brady the day before and where he had found his guilder, trying to estimate a place to start diving from the sparse details the map gave him.

'We have to take into account the westerly drift,' said Paul. 'So I reckon we should anchor about here.'

'Right,' said Jock. He swung the *Urchin* so that they would be in the best position to dive.

'Now,' said Paul to Kate, 'I want you to do exactly as you're told.'

'Why?' said Kate.

'Because we're going to do something very important and you'll have to help by keeping a log of distances and depths.' Paul produced a pencil and notebook.

'Oh,' said Kate. Paul's bossiness and sense of importance annoyed her. He made it seem that it was a favour to have her there at all. Paul handed her the maps.

'And mind those.' He got up to throw the anchor out. Then the trouble started. As he did so he accidentally bumped Kate, who had moved to get into a better position to manage the maps and the notebook.

'Watch out!' she said. She retaliated by giving Paul a shove with more force than she meant. He was thrown off balance and nearly fell, letting go of the anchor. It went in with a splash. Paul was very annoyed.

'If you're going to do that sort of thing,' he said, 'you'll stay home next time.'

'You can't act like a brat when you're out in a boat,' said Jock, getting into the fight. Kate was furious that the boys were picking on her. She got so mad that she grabbed Paul's maps.

'It was your fault in the first place,' she said. 'Take what you said back or I'll chuck your maps into the water.' And by the look of it she meant it. She had them dangling over the edge.

'Stop her!' shouted Paul. Jock made a grab to get the maps.

'You have to say you're sorry for calling me a brat,' Kate said, holding the maps tantalisingly just above the surface of the sea.

'You're proving you're a brat,' said Jock. 'Hand the maps back.'

'Not until you say you're sorry.'

The row was developing so that neither Kate nor the boys noticed a fishing boat off the point of Geelup Cove and now entering the bay.

'Kate! Behave or I'll have to tell Dad when we get home.'

Kate was incensed. Paul was using the unforgivable threat. She decided she'd really teach him a lesson and was about to throw his maps into the water when some instinct made her look up. Suddenly she saw, only a short distance away, a large, powerful fishing boat, heading straight for them and showing no sign of swerving. It was on a collision course. It would smash right into their little dinghy, knife them through, disintegrate them. Kate screamed.

'Paul! Paul! There's a boat! A boat!'

Paul swivelled around, and did a double-take, seeing the fishing boat for the first time. Desperately he tried to pull up the anchor.

'Pull up the anchor!' Jock shouted.

'It's coming straight for us!' Kate screamed. Paul was desperately yanking and tugging at the anchor rope. But the anchor wouldn't budge.

'It's caught on the reef!'

'Cut it! Cut it!' shouted Jock.

He was beside Paul now, trying to help. Paul managed to get out the fishing knife in the box near him. He hacked desperately at the anchor line. The great overwhelming bow of the boat was practically above them. They were going to be smashed to bits. Kate covered her eyes. She couldn't look. She daren't look. The roar of the fishing boat's powerful engine filled her ears. Then she felt a violent thrust. She hit the water. She went down deep, deep. At the bottom she managed to kick and turn and then the buoyancy of her life jacket brought her to the surface. She took a deep breath. Above her was the clear sky. She looked around. There was Paul. She felt an enormous sense of relief.

'Kate! Kate!' Paul was calling her anxiously. And beside him, treading water, was Jock. And, miraculously, the *Urchin* was still intact, calmly floating on the sea.

From the deck of the *Isabella* Vim, the owner of the fishing boat that had come so close to causing a tragedy, was looking down in horror at the three kids and the *Urchin*.

'Are you O.K?' he shouted, anxiety in his voice, his face strained. Jock was bobbing around in the water.

'We're all right. But you scared the hell out of us!'

Vim laughed with relief.

'And you scared the hell out of me!' he replied. 'Anyway, you'd better come aboard so that I can make sure.'

Vim leant over and grabbed Kate as she swam to the side of the boat. He helped her on deck. Then he gave a hand to the boys. Once they were on deck he again questioned them with concern.

'Are you sure you're all right?'

'Yes. We're O.K. It's nothing,' Kate said spiritedly. But her teeth were beginning to chatter and she was shivering.

'I'm not so sure,' said Vim. 'You need to be dried off and have something warm to drink.' He noticed that the boys too were shivering as a result of delayed shock and their sudden immersion and fright.

'Come into the cabin,' he said. The kids needed to restore their body warmth quickly.

With a smile Vim ushered them into the living quarters of his boat. Once inside he quickly found towels and they dried themselves. He hauled out a couple of old pullovers and windcheaters as well.

'A bit big,' he said. 'But they'll do.'

Kate nearly disappeared inside Vim's pullover.

'You look like a mouse in that,' he said.

Kate smiled at him. She liked him.

'Let's see – you're Kate, aren't you?' Vim asked. '. . . I've seen you before.'

'Yes,' said Kate. 'And that's Paul, my brother, and Jock – he's our friend,' indicating Jock huddled in a towel and one of Vim's windcheaters.

'Do you do everything together?' said Vim.

'Yes – most of the time, unless they get really bossy,' said Kate.

'You need to be bossed around sometimes,' said Jock.

'I do not, Jock Dixon!' Kate said indignantly.

Vim laughed as he started hunting through his pantry cupboard.

'I think it's time for cocoa if I can find some. I know I've got coffee.'

'Coffee will be O.K., thanks,' said Paul politely. He really felt annoyed with the others. Did they have to start a fight in front of someone they didn't know? You couldn't rely on those two. He felt embarrassed.

Vim's boat, in fact, awed all three of them. They were very impressed. It was trim and well fitted. Compared with the rough fishing craft that worked from Falcon Island, Vim's boat was a floating palace, but with an appealing homely appearance as well. There were books lying on one bunk and cushions on another, and charts attached to the sides of the cabin, and a small collection of seashells mounted in a glass case.

Paul thought it was magnificent. He'd do anything to have a boat like this when he was older. Jock was equally impressed. He began to ask Vim eager questions.

'Is that a dual steering system – wheelhouse and deck?'

'That's right,' said Vim.

'Wow!' said Jock. Then he noticed a small television set built in on one wall.

'Gosh – have you got TV too?'

'Yes,' said Vim.

'Colour?' asked Kate.

'Yes,' said Vim, laughing again. He tapped Kate playfully on the nose as he put a sugar bowl on the fold-down table.

'Great!' said Jock. 'But how do you run it? Where do you get the power?'

'I've got a 240-volt auxiliary motor.'

'Fantastic!'

'Lots of boats have them,' said Vim. 'And as I live on my boat it might as well be comfortable.'

'It's absolutely fantastic!' said Jock.

Then the whistle on the kettle started to sing. Vim turned it off and made the coffee.

'Here you are, kids.' He handed them each a mug and then opened a tin of biscuits. Paul took a grateful sip.

'Beginning to feel better?' he asked.

Kate nodded. 'Yes, thanks.'

Paul was finding that his initial impression of Vim, gained from what he had observed of him around the island, was beginning to change. He had seen Vim on the jetty once or twice, and on several occasions he had met him in the store when he had been buying provisions from Mrs Yates. Vim had seemed reserved and distant. Few people seemed to know much about him. He seemed unwilling to be drawn into the island community, and had refused invitations to go to badminton or to join the darts club when people had asked.

Vim projected a sense of remoteness, as cool as his blue eyes – the eyes of a sailor. Paul felt Vim should be on the high seas, not grubbing around in the small bays of Falcon Island, pulling nets and getting the deck of his boat filthy with fish and guts and scales.

But now he seemed much less remote. Paul came to the conclusion that maybe Vim was one of those people who seemed withdrawn until you got to know them better.

Vim had just shown Jock the automatic pilot.

'You set it on the course you want. Then no worries. It steers the boat and you get on with your work. That is,' Vim added with a laugh, 'unless you find another boat on collision course! Gosh, I got a shock when out of the blue I saw you three kids! Anyway, what were you doing so far out on the reef?'

'We were going . . .' Paul was about to say that they were going fishing, wanting to keep their intention of searching for guilders secret, but Kate beat him to it.

'We were going to search for old Dutch guilders.'

'What?' said Vim, with a strange expression on his face.

'Paul's got a guilder,' Kate said.

'Has he?' said Vim. 'Have you got it here?'

Paul rather reluctantly fished for the coin in his pocket.

'Go on. Hurry up. Show it to Vim,' urged Kate.

Paul handed his precious guilder to Vim.

'Did you find it here?' Vim asked.

'Yes. In Geelup Cove,' Paul said.

'Interesting,' said Vim.

Vim examined the coin as if it were something special.

'Just a second,' he said. He leant past Jock and opened a small cupboard above a bunk. Inside there were a variety of instruments and racks of small tools. In addition there was a microscope, and several stoppered bottles that apparently contained chemicals and some glass beakers.

'My workshop,' Vim said. 'I'm interested in old things that come from the sea bed too.'

He selected a tool – a small scalpel with a flat spatula blade at one end – and a magnifying glass. He began to scrape the surface of the coin.

'There's a lot of concretion,' he said.

'What's concretion?' Paul was peering over his shoulder, now a bit breathless. What if it proved not to be a guilder after all?

'Concretion is the name given to the hard build-up on objects that have been in the ocean for a long time. It's the effect of sea water and corrosion on metal over a considerable period.'

Vim's absorption in his task of cleaning part of the coin almost seemed to exclude the kids. Jock and Kate looked on with interest. Paul waited with bated breath. At last Vim scraped a patch of the coin clean. Paul was surprised to see a definite look of disappointment cross his face.

'Well . . . for a minute . . . I thought maybe. . . . He shook his head as he handed the coin to Paul. 'I'm sorry, Paul. It's only an old two-shilling piece. You see?' He showed Paul the edge of the coin under the magnifying glass. 'There. It's got a milled edge. Serrations. None of the very old Dutch coins had that edge to them. Bad luck!'

Paul was so disappointed that he could hardly speak. Then he managed to say, 'Are you sure?'

'Absolutely sure,' said Vim. 'See? I'll show you.'

He took a wooden casket down from the cupboard where his tools were kept. He opened it. Inside were a number of coins, and pieces of pewter and silver, most of them worn, frail and incomplete from the action of the sea and time. But Vim handled them carefully, almost reverently.

'There's a silver guilder,' he said, showing Kate and

Paul and Jock. The coin that lay in his hand was small with a deeply stamped design of a bearded Emperor. Paul's coin was much larger and quite different.

'Oh,' said Paul. He had to admit it. His coin wasn't a guilder after all.

'And here are other Dutch coins,' said Vim. 'This is a thaler.' It too was a small silver coin. 'And a stuyver – that's another kind of old Dutch coin, and this one . . .' he handled the coin very carefully as he showed it to the kids, '. . . is very special. It's a Rix dollar also from the same period.'

'Did they have dollars then?' said Jock.

'Yes,' said Vim.

He began to put the coins back in the case.

'Did you find the guilder here?' asked Paul.

'No. In the Islands – near Djakarta in Indonesia. That's where the Dutch East India Company had its head-quarters. All the Dutch ships lost on the western coast were Dutch East India Company ships.'

'Yeah. We've learnt all about it at school,' said Kate.

Vim put the box away in the cupboard.

'Well, that's that,' he said. 'For a second there I must admit you gave me another shock. I thought you'd found what I've been looking for.'

'I don't understand,' Jock said.

'The *Golden Falcon*. I've been looking for it.'

'You've been looking for it!' Paul exclaimed.

'Yeah. For ages. But those dead men don't give up their secrets so easily. They're selfish, those old Dutch-men!' He seemed to say it almost with affection.

'And I thought for a moment you'd beaten me to it. I've been diving and searching everywhere. But so far – nothing!'

'Nothing at all?' asked Paul with concealed excitement.

'Nothing,' said Vim.

'Diving with a snorkel?' said Jock.

'No.' Vim laughed. 'You can't explore properly with a

snorkel. I've been scuba diving – with a wet suit and an air tank. Exploring. But I haven't found a thing. Maybe the *Golden Falcon* doesn't exist. Maybe it's a legend after all.'

Paul was eagerly digging deeper into his shorts. He found the pieces of bone.

'What about these?' Paul said.

'They're bones. Sailors' bones,' said Kate.

'What?' exclaimed Vim. 'You're full of surprises, you kids!'

Paul quickly passed Vim his pieces of bone. Vim picked up the magnifying glass again. He studied the objects carefully. He scraped the surface with the scalpel. Then he shook his head.

'Sorry, Paul. It's coral. Only old sun-baked coral. It's not bone.'

All Paul's dreams were destroyed at once. Everything that he'd built up in his mind vanished as a sandcastle on the beach vanishes with the first onrush of the tide. He looked out of the porthole, turning his head. He didn't dare look at the others. Tears were welling up in his eyes. He brushed them away, feeling ashamed. He looked out at the gently lapping water of Geelup Cove, and the white sandhills and sharp white limestone ridges above them. So much had happened since this time yesterday. He had been convinced that they would unravel the secret of the *Golden Falcon*. Perhaps now they never would.

Paul became lost in his thoughts. He didn't pay much attention to the conversation Jock and Vim were having. Vim showed Jock and Kate more details of his boat, the sonar equipment, the compass, his shower and laundry area. He kept Jock and Kate out of the way until Paul had had time to recover. He was aware of Paul's great disappointment. Vim himself knew how deep disappointment could be.

Jock, Vim and Kate came back into the cabin from the

forward section. Paul heard Jock say, 'You'll let us have a go at steering?'

'Sure.'

'Wow!'

'And Kate, and you too, Paul, if you like,' said Vim, smiling.

'Oh! Oh – yeah!' said Paul, recovering. 'That'd be great!'

'O.K., then let's get underway,' Vim said.

Vim helped them free the *Urchin*'s anchor. Then they secured the *Urchin* to the stern of the Isabella. Vim started the diesel motor. With Vim standing close and guiding them, Jock, Kate and Paul took it in turns to bring Vim's boat, with the *Urchin* in tow, out of Geelup Cove and around the promontory and Wireless Hill towards the town jetty. Jock felt he was really someone special as he manoeuvred the powerful boat and brought her into the jetty.

As it happened, on this particular afternoon the jetty was almost deserted. The only person there was Mrs Yates, who came down each evening with left-over bread to feed the seagulls.

Jock, still at the controls of the *Isabella*, was disappointed. He'd hoped for a much bigger audience that would notice and be impressed with the smooth way that he handled the *Isabella*.

'Throttle her back now,' said Vim, taking over.

Paul leapt off and secured the mooring line. Mrs Yates, surrounded by a flock of voracious screeching seagulls, was surprised to see the kids on Vim's boat, but responded suitably.

'Very nice, Jock!' she called.

Jock felt satisfied.

But then it was time to go. They gave Vim back his pullover and windcheaters.

'Bye, Vim! Thanks,' the kids said. 'See you.'

'Bye, kids!' said Vim. 'See you soon, O.K.?'

'Right,' they said.

Jock, Paul and Kate left the jetty. All the fishing boats were back, swinging and rocking at their moorings. And Brady's boat too was tied up in its usual place.

'Brady's back,' said Paul.

'Yeah,' said Jock noncommittally.

After a pause he said, 'Do you think Vim'll keep his promise?'

'What promise?'

'To teach us to dive!' Jock said.

'I didn't hear him say that.'

'You were looking out of the porthole. But you must've heard.'

'No.'

'Well, anyway – he's got a spare wet suit. If we can get another one he'll teach us to dive with tanks and everything.

'And me,' said Kate.

'Gee – that'd be great!' said Paul. 'Does he want us to help him find the *Golden Falcon*?'

'You never think about anything but that old wreck!' Jock said. 'I reckon you're obsessed. Yeah, obsessed.' Jock felt very pleased with that word. Paul flushed. To Jock, learning to dive – not kids' stuff with snorkels, but properly with air tanks – was a fantastic idea. Something new. Something different. No other kids on Falcon Island could scuba dive.

They were now crossing the jetty car park. Paul was trying to think of something that would put Jock back in his place when he heard a noise, a voice. But it sounded all wrong. Somebody was singing, 'My old man's a dustman, a dustman. . . .' Then the voice trailed off.

Then it tried again, in a slightly higher key, 'My old man's a dustman. . . .'

'Who's that?' whispered Kate.

Then from behind a parked car emerged Brady, with his hat on one side and his tie askew.

'Good afternoon, kids!' he said, sweeping off his hat.

The kids stood mesmerised.

'Nice day,' Brady added. He did a bit of a hop and a skip and a bow. The bow ended with a decidedly uncertain wobble. He gave a little chuckle. Then he went in the direction of his truck, 'My old man's a dustman . . .'

Kate was the first to find her voice.

'Brady had better watch out,' she said, 'or Constable Harris will get him, and he'll be sorry!'

'What's he been celebrating?' said Jock.

'Dunno,' said Paul in amazement.

It looked as if Brady had just won the Million Dollar Lottery.

Chapter 4

During the next few days Brady's uncharacteristic behaviour was the subject of considerable gossip and speculation. The unexpected good humour that the children had experienced when they met him in the car park seemed to be no passing phase. Brady was suddenly saying 'good day' to people in the street, tipping his hat to the ladies, and buying a few rounds at the pub. Mrs Mortimer said that she even heard him crack a joke. This was unprecedented. 'Brady hasn't cracked a joke since Adam was a boy,' said Harry in the Post Office. What was it all about? Why this sudden change?

There were even bets on several ideas – that Brady had won at the races, or maybe he was in love. The latter idea was pretty quickly dropped. Brady in love seemed very unlikely. Maybe he had won the Pools. Most people came to the conclusion that he must have inherited some money. Whatever it was Brady wasn't going to say, and he continued for the rest of the week in an unnatural state of good humour.

Mrs Yates regarded the whole matter darkly.

'Miracles have been known to happen before,' she said to Mrs Pike one afternoon when the kids were in the shop. 'But I wouldn't like the wind to change.'

'What does she mean by that?' Kate said.

'She reckons that Brady's politeness and everything won't last for long,' said Jock.

All the fuss extended even to the kids at school. They talked about nothing else but Brady.

Kate asked Miss Fitzgerald, 'Do you think Mr Brady's been left some money?'

Miss Fitzgerald, aware that whatever the teacher said might be regarded as an authoritative opinion, was cautious.

'Well, if he has, wouldn't it be a good thing?'

Miss Fitzgerald knew that many of the islanders lived close to the breadline, supporting themselves by catering for summer tourists, but when summer ended there wasn't much work, and then there was hardship. Each year a few families had to leave the island to find jobs on the mainland. Jack Brady was one of those who scratched a living by occasionally working at the hotel, delivering stores brought in by the ferry, and fishing when the fish were running. It wasn't an easy life and every cent counted.

But by the end of the week Brady had started to revert to his normal state of irritability and bad temper, and the islanders turned to other things. Mrs Yates, however, wasn't quite ready to drop the matter. She let it slip that Brady was getting pamphlets in the mail about new cars, and holidays in Hawaii and Japan and other places, and that he was getting brochures about new boats, but the islanders weren't very interested any more. Everyone was now talking about Mr Meredith, who had fallen off a ladder while mending his roof and had to be taken at high speed by water ambulance to the mainland to have a gash in his leg sewn up.

But Paul was still thinking about Brady. He kept quietly wondering. What had been in Brady's canvas bag? Brady had been carrying it that evening in the car park, and Paul was sure it had been empty. Kate had said there were lots of packets, and they were numbered. Why? Why should he number packets of sand and then take them all the way to the mainland and not bring them back? It didn't make sense. Maybe Brady was going to put down a bore for water? But nobody would bore for water in the sand dunes. To Paul, Brady's behaviour was as frustrating as having two jigsaw puzzles mixed up in one box. Nothing fitted together in a coherent way.

Jock had soon forgotten about Brady. The big thing to him was that Vim was continuing with his plans to teach them to dive.

On Tuesday evening at tea, Paul asked Frank if they could learn to scuba dive with Vim. Frank was immediately enthusiastic.

'A good idea,' he said. 'It'll give you kids something really interesting to do. And he's a nice bloke, that young Dutchman!'

Paul was surprised. 'Is he Dutch?'

'Yes,' said Frank. 'Vim is short for Wilhelm. The Dutch people pronounce a "W" as a "V".'

'What's his full name?' Paul said.

'Wilhelm Van Doren – couldn't get anything more Dutch than that.'

'Oh,' said Paul thoughtfully, remembering the affectionate, almost possessive way in which Vim had referred to the old Dutch sailors when he'd shown them his guilder and the silver and pewter bowls he had found in Java. And that was probably why he had named his boat *Isabella* – the same name as the sister boat to the *Golden Falcon*.

'He doesn't sound Dutch,' said Kate.

'He's probably been here for a long time,' said Frank.

This was Kate's first question when they went down to the jetty a few days later. Vim was coming off his boat, striding along, carrying a fishing net, looking like an old-world sailor – tall, blue-eyed and with a glinting gold ear ring in one ear. Kate ran to meet him.

'Vim, are you really Dutch?' she asked.

The naturalness of Kate's curiosity made Vim laugh.

'Yes, I am. I was born in Holland. I came to Australia when I was younger than you, Kate.'

'Well, I'm eight,' said Kate.

'I was five.'

'Can you speak Dutch?'

Paul beside them felt a little embarrassed.

'*Ja. Natuurlijk kan ik dat, jonge dame.*'

'What does that mean?'

'Yes, of course I can, pretty little Miss.' Vim playfully tweaked Kate's pigtails. Kate and Paul followed Vim across the beach to the place where he spread out his fishing nets to dry.

'That's fantastic! He's really Dutch!' she said to Paul. 'He can speak it.'

Paul, more embarrassed, wished she'd stop talking like that. But Vim only laughed. These kids! It was like having blondeheaded brothers and sister all over again. That sort of bond had been missing in his life for a long time.

Then Kate said, 'When are you going to teach us to dive? Jock's Grandpop is buying him a wet suit, the lucky thing.'

Vim suddenly felt stricken. He gathered Kate into a hug.

'Sorry, Katey,' he said. 'Not you.'

'Not me!' said Kate. 'Why?' Suddenly the warm sunshine seemed to disappear and the beach felt cold and windswept. Vim, Paul could see, was unhappy and distressed. Kate searched Vim's face. Although Vim was upset, he meant what he said.

'You're too little, *kleintje*, you couldn't carry the air tank. It just isn't possible. When you're bigger.'

Kate wanted to cry. She couldn't remember having felt so disappointed in her life before. She bit her lip. She didn't want Vim to think she was a baby.

'But you can come with us and watch,' Vim said.

'That's not the same,' she said.

Vim still looked very sympathetic but he said, 'Sorry, Katey, that's the way it is.'

Sadly Kate had to accept. However she had overcome much of her disappointment by the following Saturday morning when Paul and Jock went for their first diving lesson. Jock's grandparents had bought him a wet suit. It was black rubber with a zip-up front. He had a mask, the mouthpiece, fins, the air tank – everything. Paul felt a little touch of envy but he didn't comment. Sometimes Jock's grandparents bought Jock a lot of things to make up for the fact that his parents were divorced and neither parent really wanted him to live with them. And that had a lot to do with the way Jock like to live every day in the present and didn't want to look back on things very much. Now he was so proud. His face was beaming.

'Aren't they great?' he said.

'Yes,' said Paul, and he meant it quite genuinely. His father had bought him fins and mask and mouthpiece, and had promised him a wet suit for his birthday.

Kate tried to lift the air tank. It was so heavy that she could only just lift it up. She now realised that she wasn't old enough yet to go diving – she wasn't big enough or strong enough. But she felt happy to be included.

'It's all great,' said Kate.

'Ready, kids?' said Vim.

Their first lessons took place on the beach. Kate lay in the sand, near flat rocks covered with shells, pointed winkles and barnacles. The sea came lapping in over the rocks in a lazy way.

The boys were having to concentrate. There were a number of very important things they had to learn. Vim showed them the air tank. He indicated the gauge with numbers on it.

'This shows the air pressure in the tank,' he said. 'There must be no less than seventy per cent air in the tank at all times. You have to keep a check on that. It's vital to your safety when you're under water.'

Then he took them through the procedures relating to the breathing regulator. He got Jock to put the regulator in his mouth. Then Paul had to listen carefully to check if there were any slight hissing sounds that would indicate an air leak in the connection between the air regulator and the tank.

'No. No air leaks,' Paul said.

'Good,' said Vim.

Then he made Jock go through the same routine.

Next they had to prepare their face masks. Vim demonstrated.

'You have to spit in the mask and then wipe the spit around the glass.'

'Yuk!' said Kate.

'It stops the mask from misting up under water,' Vim said.

He checked that the boys had done this properly.

Next Vim took them through the underwater signals. He put his arm at a right angle to his body, with his forearm and finger pointing.

'What does that mean?'

'Going up,' said Paul.

'Good,' said Vim. 'That's right.'

'Now, what does this mean?' Vim threw his arm straight up in the air.

Paul hesitated but Jock answered at once.

'Help. I'm in trouble.'

'That's right. . . . You've been studying the book I gave you, I can see. Now, Paul – what about this one?'

Vim pressed his closed fist to his chest.

'Out of air!' said Jock smartly.

'Low on air!' Paul said at the same time.

'Paul's right,' said Vim.

From then on Vim made them go through the drill on the underwater signals again and again until neither Paul nor Jock, nor Kate, who was joining in from the sidelines, made any mistakes. Vim was absolutely firm that they had to know every routine thoroughly before he would even let them go on his boat.

But eventually he was satisfied.

'O.K.,' he said. 'Now we can try the real thing.'

Carrying their gear the boys, followed by Kate, ran along the jetty. Their footsteps over the rough planking woke up Mr Meredith, who had been pretending to fish but was, in fact, having a quiet doze in the sun.

'What's going on?' he mumbled, then – 'Diving! Wish I were younger. I'd come too.'

The kids clambered on to the *Isabella*. Then Vim took the boat out around the bay and into Geelup Cove. As always the reef sheltered the beach and the water was calm and as clear as glass.

There were more things to learn. Vim checked their suits and weight belts again, saying as he did, 'In choppy water the best thing to do is a back roll. But today the conditions are perfect, so we will go in feet first. You never dive in head first when you are wearing diving gear – you would dislodge your mask straight away. Ready now?' Vim stood up. 'I'll show you.'

As the kids watched, Vim, in his wet suit and mask and fins, went to the stern of the *Isabella*. Holding one hand firmly against his mask so that it wouldn't dislodge with the impact of hitting the water, he jumped in. As the kids watched through the clear water they saw him go to the bottom, a series of bubbles following him. Vim swam along the ocean floor for a moment, then surfaced and came back to the boat. Jock and Paul helped him aboard.

'Did you see what I did?'

'Yes,' they said.

'Right. Now you. But first . . .' he raised a hand before they pulled on their masks, 'What is the most important rule to follow?'

'Always stick together,' they said.

'That's right,' said Vim. 'Make sure you remember it.'

Standing on the deck Paul suddenly felt a great thrill of

challenge and adventure mixed with nervousness. But he was determined to prove that he could do it. Vim went in first, then Jock. Jock had been quite jaunty before he dived, but had he too been feeling anxious and hiding his fears with an act of bravado? Paul could see them both, two dark fluid shapes beneath the water. His heart was pounding. He had to go. He put his hand against his mask. He could feel the comforting deck of the boat beneath his feet. What would it be like? It seemed a long way down. He hesitated. Would he be able to breathe properly? He felt himself poised suspended in indecision. But. . . .

Now! He flipped backwards and hit the water. Surprisingly it was cold. Water rushed inside his wet suit. He could feel the bubbles of air passing his face. Then the water inside his wet suit started to warm up. He was floating, he was free, he was suspended in time. He just wanted to drift. He could breathe! It was better, much better than the snorkel that he had used in diving for so long; he felt that he could soar and plunge and dive. He was fascinated by the air bubbles. He wanted to play with them, chase them. But then Vim was beside him, circling him. He looked strangely remote behind his mask. And yet Vim hovered about him as if anxious and wanting to be reassured. Paul gave him the O.K. signal. Vim signalled him to swim beside him, to join Jock who was treading water. Paul felt that he was part of the sea. Then together they began to explore the variety, wonder and beauty of the reef, gently parting long ribbons of sea kelp that hung in the entrance to the largest underwater cave, entering the secret hidden domain of the sea creatures of the Cove.

That afternoon they returned to the town jetty, tired but happy. They had collected a number of sea treasures, operculums and sea urchins, clams and red coral. They were determined that they would dive again as soon as they could. It had been a wonderful day.

Vim went with them to the store. The children were hungry. They wanted a bag of chips, and Vim wanted some things too.

Mrs Yates was very happy to see them.

'You all look very pleased with yourselves,' she said.

'Vim's teaching us to dive,' said Jock.

'Learning to dive!' said Mrs Yates. 'Why, what a wonderful idea!'

As she spoke the bell on the door rang. Someone else had come into the store – Jack Brady. But Mrs Yates continued to be interested in Jock.

'Diving!' she said. 'Do you go down to the depths? Fancy – you could meet the denizens of the deep,' she added.

Vim and Paul and Kate and Jock laughed.

'We only go down about five metres,' said Vim. 'But that's deep enough.'

Brady was looking very impatient. He tapped the counter. Mrs Yates ignored him.

'Do you mind. . . .' he said.

Mrs Yates appeared not to notice. She was really taken with the diving.

'Well, you never know,' she said. 'If you learn to dive really well, one day you might find the *Golden Falcon*. It's out there in deep water somewhere. I know it is. And one day it will be found – perhaps you'll find it, Paulie.'

Christopher! Paul thought, blushing. Calling me Paulie. What will Vim think. But Vim winked at Paul, and smiling said, 'Maybe. . . .'

But he didn't have a chance to finish. Brady had had enough.

'Are you serving?' he said to Mrs Yates belligerently. 'Or are you going to stand there all day talking absolute rot and rubbish about the imaginary wreck.'

Mrs Yates bridled instantly.

'You watch your language in my shop, Jack Brady,' she said. 'And the *Golden Falcon* is not imaginary!'

Brady apparently saw no need to apologise.

'I haven't got all day,' he said. 'Do you or don't you have some spuds?'

'Do you mean potatoes?' said Mrs Yates haughtily.

'I mean spuds,' said Brady.

'I only sell potatoes,' said Mrs Yates.

'Don't you know what a spud is, you silly old bag?' said Brady.

'Potatoes,' said Mrs Yates.

It was going to be stalemate. Vim, looking startled, decided that he wasn't going to stay to see who would win. He ushered the kids out of the shop.

'For heaven's sake,' he said.

The kids laughed. 'That's nothing. Mrs Yates and Brady always go on like that,' Jock said.

'And he won't get his potatoes unless he says potatoes,' said Kate.

'Mrs Yates never lets him get away with anything,' said Paul. 'It makes old Brady really as wild as hell.'

'She's something to reckon with,' said Vim. 'Anyway,' he said, changing the subject, 'do you want to come diving again next weekend?'

The kids' faces lit up.

'Sure,' they said.

'That's arranged then,' said Vim.

Chapter 5

When the following Saturday came, Jock was around early helping Kate and Paul pack things for their day out on Vim's boat. Jock had brought tomatoes and grapes from Nan's garden, which were soon placed in a large box along with hard-boiled eggs, bread rolls, cold meat and a fruit cake that Kate had made.

Then Frank sent Kate to her bedroom for a shady hat.

'No burnt noses,' he said. 'Have you got sunburn cream?'

'Yes,' said Paul.

'Goodbye then,' said Frank, watching them go.

Kate hurried along with the boys; she was so happy bouncing along with her pigtails swinging as she chattered beside them. They were really very good to her. They were lucky kids – all three of them, Frank thought.

Vim was waiting at the jetty.

'Hi!' he said.

'Hi, Vim!'

Within a few minutes they were leaving the bay, the powerful thrust of the boat's engine churning. The seagulls that used the *Isabella* for a perch when she was moored followed them for a distance until they rounded the promontory at Wireless Hill and entered Geelup Cove. As Vim eased back the throttle, the *Isabella* slid through the gap in the reef. The cove was deserted, the white beach curved away from them, the waves lapped on the beach lazily, the air was light and clear. It was a perfect summer day.

'Right. Anchor!' instructed Vim. Paul and Jock threw

out the anchor. They were in the middle section of the reef where it was sheltered but the water was a reasonable depth.

Vim made the boys go through their drills again. He was making quite sure that their responses to his commands were fast and accurate.

'What does "arm up", mean?'

'I need help – come and get me.'

'Right. What does a clenched fist mean?'

'I have opened my air reserve.'

'What does pointing to my watch mean?'

'Time is running out. Time to go up,' said the boys.

'Good,' said Vim, finally satisfied. 'Now we can kit up and go down to see what's on the reef today.'

Within minutes all three of them were in the water going down to the deepest cave in Geelup Cove. On the *Isabella* Kate was content to lie in the sun with a comic and drowse until they returned.

Under water, Vim led them through the deepest cave into an inner cavern. At first it was a little dark. It took a moment or two for Paul's eyes to adjust, but then what he saw fascinated him. Small silver fish darted past, followed by a large groper in lazy pursuit of a meal. Paul saw Jock indicating to look in his direction. Paul almost wanted to laugh, a thing he couldn't do very well with the mask over his face and the snorkel in his mouth.

Near Jock a small octopus had been jetting along with no apparent cares until he saw them. The small octopus stopped. His tentacles waved in the water in indecision. Should he, he seemed to wonder, come and investigate these large creatures or should he bolt for safety? He hung there in the sea, almost as if he were scratching his head. Suddenly turning bright red he made up his mind. He decided caution would be the better thing, and he propelled himself fast into a neat rock crevice not far from Jock's legs. Paul could see his beady little eyes sticking out, watching them, prepared to stare, now that he was safe. Their interest in the octopus was diverted by Vim indicating that they should come and see a flathead, a fish lying on the sandy bottom. Its colouring matched the bottom so well that it was almost impossible to make out the fish from the rocks and sand.

Altogether the life on the reef was completely fascinating. But nevertheless Paul kept looking for something – some sort of evidence that might prove the whereabouts of the *Golden Falcon*. Even though his guilder had turned out to be an ordinary Australian florin, he still hoped that they might solve the secret of the wreck.

After a while Vim signalled that they must surface. He wasn't going to let them stay down too long. And, besides, he was thinking of Kate, alone on the boat. Once back on board he would take them out to Seal Rocks to see the seal colony there, so that there would be something of interest for Kate too.

And this was the pattern that developed over the next few weeks. They went diving on most Saturday and Sunday afternoons. Sometimes Kate came and sometimes she stayed at home with Frank or went to play with her friend Wendy.

Within a very short time Jock and Paul were on the way to becoming proficient divers.

On the fourth Sunday Kate came with them. It was very hot. The past few days had been mild, but by nine o'clock on this particular day the temperature was climbing fast. It was going to be a scorcher.

Vim was ready for them when they all trooped down to the jetty.

'Geelup Cove?' Jock asked as they piled on board. Sometimes recently they had been to Settler's Bay where the water was shallow and the conditions safe, but mostly they went to Geelup Cove.

'Yes, Geelup Cove,' said Vim. For a moment it seemed as if he was going to say something else, but he changed his mind. Paul cast off the mooring line and they set off. The *Isabella* was now as familiar to them as if it were their own. It seemed like part of their lives, and it seemed as if Vim had always been their friend.

They anchored in the usual place in Geelup Cove, and within minutes they were in their wet suits and over the side, descending into the dreamy world of the floor of the sea.

Straightaway Vim saw a crayfish and decided that he would get it. But the crayfish had other ideas and backed into the rock crevice that it had been resting on. Vim plunged his arm into the crevice, determined to get the crayfish for lunch.

Jock was beside Vim, Paul nearby. Paul was examining sea urchins attached to a coral face. There was one in particular that caught his attention. The surface was striped with dark markings, in the centre of which were tiny patches of brilliant red, like glowing red velvet. Paul was tempted to take it, but he knew that its colours would fade when it was taken out of the water. It was beautiful while it lived. Then something else caught his eye. It was a seahorse; Father seahorse with a family of small seahorses, all replicas of himself. Entranced, Paul followed them as they swam along the reef.

Jock, who had been near Paul, and had been investigating a hermit crab in a turban shell, saw Paul swim away from him, but he wasn't worried. Paul knew that it was almost time to surface. Jock went back to examining the hermit crab who was sitting like an old woman with her knitting, stroking her furry legs in the entrance of the shell.

Paul, not aware of how far he was going, followed the seahorse family, intrigued by the way the babies kept perfect formation behind Father. They swam some distance until the seahorses entered a large rock hollow. It was a big one, almost like a grotto. Reason told Paul to turn back, but suddenly, beyond the seahorses, he saw, half buried in the sand, a round encrusted shape, almost concealed by fronds of seaweed. His heart started to beat quickly. A foreign object. Was it a relic? It had obviously been in the water for a long time. Perhaps – he only allowed himself to half believe it – but perhaps it just might be something from the *Golden Falcon*. Excitedly he swam towards it.

The hermit crab that had fascinated Jock decided abruptly that it was bored with visitors and retreated back into the depths of its shell. Jock looked around. Where was Paul? Vim had won his tussle with the crayfish, and had also got a second one which he put in his dive bag. Just the very thing for lunch. He checked his watch. Time to go up.

Then Vim became aware of Jock, at the entrance of the cavern, signalling trouble. Vim turned fast. Shark? No. Jock with cramp? No. Jock seemed all right. But where was Paul? Vim controlled his sudden onrush of alarm. He couldn't see Paul anywhere. He swam to Jock.

Jock was indicating that Paul had swum out of the grotto – but in which direction? Vim looked around quickly. Paul was nowhere in the immediate vicinity. That meant that he must have gone out towards the far end of the reef, where he had been told often enough that he must not go alone. Vim's anxiety was instantly mixed with anger. Paul had no right to disobey him.

Vim indicated that Jock was to surface at once, taking the dive bag. Jock hesitated. He, too, was frightened. Where was Paul? But Vim's instructions were firm. Vim couldn't have the worry of two youngsters on his mind at the same time. Jock was to surface and he was to go to the boat. Jock took the dive bag and began to swim towards the anchor rope of the *Isabella* ten metres away. Vim watched him until he saw him near the anchor rope, then, very worried, he turned to search for Paul.

Vim swam fast along the edge of the reef, beating the water in a quick and urgent rhythm. Most of the caves were small and could be easily checked. Paul was not in any of the most immediate ones. Vim, sick at heart, swam on, his fins beating through the water. His change of pace caused a flurry in the sea creatures. Quick movement in water indicates danger. The fish and the eels and the crabs all darted to places of safety as Vim swam. Vim entered a further large cave. Still no Paul.

Paul, unaware of the anxiety he was causing, and unaware that the air level gauge on his air tank was starting to approach the danger level, was trying to prise the concreted object that he had found away from the reef. He'd had to clear the weed, and he had to scrape and gouge at the object which had become lodged between two rocks. Finally he managed to tug it free. He felt a great glow of satisfaction. He examined the object carefully. It was round and solid, most likely made of brass, covered in concretion and barnacles. He was sure it was a valuable find, old, perhaps something from the elusive Dutch wreck. He couldn't wait to take it to Vim. Then he turned to go back. But within a few metres he wasn't sure which way to go.

Vim, still searching for Paul, was beginning to feel frightened, his anger replaced by fear. Where was Paul? Was he in trouble with his air tank? Had he got himself wedged into a rock crevice that he couldn't get out of? Vim swam through a small tunnel into a secondary grotto. Paul wasn't there. He swam out again and on. All the time, the sea creatures around him were picking up his sense of urgency and the presence of danger, and they were transmitting this from one section of the reef to the next. A school of fish fled.

Paul now had ventured into a space that seemed as if it would take him out of the caverns and into the open area of the reef. But each section was now seeming to be a maze that he couldn't escape from.

Jock had climbed up on to the deck of *Isabella*. Kate helped him up.

'Where's Paul? Where's Vim?'

Jock didn't know what to say. He scanned the water looking for their heads as they surfaced. There was nothing. Kate caught his fear.

'What's happened?'

Jock was too frightened to answer. All he could do was to shake his head and keep staring at the sea.

Vim emerged from a third grotto, beginning to feel sick. Wouldn't he ever find Paul? Suddenly to his immense relief he saw a large groper swim quickly out of a hollow, and then Paul. Vim moved fast towards him. He had never felt such relief in his life. He had found him. Thank God! Paul was safe.

Although Vim felt overwhelming relief that he had found Paul, and that Paul was safe, he was very, very angry. Up on deck he decided that Paul must be taught a lesson that he would never forget.

'You broke the rules,' Vim said.

Paul tried to explain.

'I saw these seahorses. . . .'

'But I told you never to go off alone.'

'Yes, I know,' said Paul miserably, 'But. . . .'

'It was the most important rule.'

'I know – but I saw this porthole and I thought. . . .'

Vim didn't allow him to finish.

'It's nothing,' he replied contemptuously. 'It's not old.' He threw it back into the sea.

Paul was very upset. He knew he'd been stupid, which was very humiliating, but to lose Vim's good opinion as well was unbearable.

'I'm sorry,' he said.

'I'm sorry too,' said Vim, still stern. 'I thought you were ready. Today I was going to suggest that we try something more complicated. I thought maybe we could go to Dutchman's Bay, to see if we could try to solve the secret of the *Golden Falcon* together – as a team. But that will have to wait now.'

Paul felt crushed. Kate and Jock looked very subdued and sorry for him. That made it worse.

Vim, seeing Paul's unhappy face, decided that he must relent a little.

'You were getting low on air, Paul. Did you realise that?'

Paul shook his head.

'You must always do everything properly and check every procedure when you are diving,' Vim said. 'The sea is the master – there is danger all the time, and you must remember it. But – if you do the right thing diving can be the most wonderful experience in the world.'

His face softened.

'I wonder if eventually you can prove to me that you can be trusted?'

'I will – I will!' said Paul.

'All right then – I'll take your word. But we'll have to put off serious diving in Dutchman's Bay for a while.'

With that Vim closed the matter. He felt that he had been a bit hard. But he had deliberately told Paul about his plans for diving in Dutchman's Bay to begin searching for the *Golden Falcon* so that Paul would never forget today's lesson. And Jock too. Nothing could be more important than teaching the boys the fundamental lessons of safety under water.

Now Vim decided that a change of mood was required.

'Who's hungry?' he said.

'Me,' said Jock. 'I could eat a horse!'

'Crayfish do?' said Vim.

After lunch they put an awning over the deck so that they could have a sleep in the shade. It was very hot. Within seconds they were lulled to sleep by the gentle rocking of *Isabella*. All except Paul. Although Vim seemed to have forgiven him, Paul still felt humiliation at the stupid thing he had done, and how he had come close to losing Vim's respect. He lay awake. But then the soothing rocking of the boat began to lull him as well. His eyelids began to droop. He moved a little to get more comfortable. Jock and Kate were both curled up like kittens. The deck was a bit hard. He looked out across the water. It was a shimmering blue, the sand and the rocks were a white haze, the coastal scrub a dark green blur. Suddenly Paul thought he saw a movement. A flash of colour on the sandhills. Colour? Someone was on the sandhills.

Paul moved a little to see better, squinting against the sun. There was something odd about what was happening. The person on the sandhills seemed to be hitting something. A tourist, he thought. What were they doing? In the past there had been one or two hideous cases of people clubbing defenceless wallabies. Paul quickly got up and went into the cabin to get Vim's binoculars. He trained them on the sandhill. The blob of colour was still there, and there was anthother blob of colour further up. He got the binoculars in focus. There was definitely a person there with something orange. It was Brady! Brady seemed to have a bundle of stakes with him. He was driving a stake into the sand. Then there was the flash of colour again. Brady began to unwind a reel of what appeared to be orange-coloured ribbon. What on earth was he doing? Paul watched as he tied a length of ribbon on to the stake he had driven in. That was the third. The ribbons fluttered like orange flowers in the wind. For heaven's sake! Brady must really be off his head.

'He's nuts,' said Paul aloud.

'Who's nuts?' said Jock sleepily. He'd been aware that Paul had got up and had been moving about.

'Brady!' said Paul. He was so amazed that he couldn't keep his voice down.

Vim woke up.

'What's happening?' he said.

'Brady's gone completely looney,' Paul said. 'He's tied streamers on sticks, and they're all over the sandhill.' It was ludicrous. He started to laugh.

'Looks like he's trying to decorate the island single-handed. Perhaps he's having a party or something.' He laughed again. Brady had put in the fourth ribbon-covered stick.

'Let's see,' said Vim, curious. He took the binoculars and focused them on the sandhill.

The boys were beside him. Jock was saying,

'Let me see!'

'He's bats,' said Paul.

'Go back to sleep, everybody,' mumbled Kate, protesting.

Vim was taking a long, careful look at the sandhill. His face was quite serious. He wasn't laughing.

'I think we'd better take a look at what Brady's doing,' he said.

'Why?' said Jock. 'What is it?'

'Not sure,' said Vim. 'But they look like marker pegs to me. Could be a road going in there.'

'Gosh, it would spoil Geelup Cove to have a road to the beach,' said Kate, sitting up.

'That's what I think,' said Vim. 'Let's go and see what it's all about.'

They all scrambled into Vim's dinghy and he rowed them ashore. They climbed the steep path that they were so familiar with. Brady had gone. All that remained were strangely festive stakes, with fluttering orange streamers.

'This way, Vim,' said Paul helping Vim up the track.

As they got closer they could see that what had looked like orange ribbons from a distance were, in fact, strips of orange plastic.

'They *are* marker pegs,' said Vim.

Kate was the first to reach a stake.

'This one's got paper wrapped around it,' she called.

Kate was right. That particular stake had both coloured plastic ribbons and a piece of paper firmly wound around the top of the stake and tied on with a piece of binder twine.

'It all looks like a mad Tibetan prayer flag,' said Paul, who had been studying the Himalayas in school recently.

'That wouldn't be Brady,' said Jock.

'No,' said Paul.

Vim carefully untied the binder twine and removed the piece of paper. As he read it, his face grew grave.

'What is it, Vim?' said Kate.

'It's a miner's claim,' he said.

Jock burst out into a great hoot of laughter.

'That proves it. Brady's really crazy. What is there to mine here? It's all sand.

'He had sand in those bags he took to the mainland that day,' said Paul.

'Sand in bags?' said Vim. 'What do you mean?'

'He had little bags of sand, all numbered,' said Kate. 'We saw him getting them when we were here swimming one day after school.'

'That's right,' said Paul. He explained what they had found.

'He took sand samples here?' said Vim. 'Why?'

'We don't know,' said Jock. 'He just did it. I reckon he's nuts.'

'Show me where,' said Vim.

The kids hurried up the sandhill. They got to the place where they had seen Brady the afternoon that Paul had found his coin. They started to push the sand aside with their hands, scooping it out, digging down. After they had excavated about half a metre, they discovered the same sort of sand that Brady had had in his packets. Black sand.

Vim looked down at the hole. Then he knelt down and picked up some of the sand. It was heavy and shiny and black.

'Black beach sand,' he said. At once he understood what that might mean. Ilmenite. A beach sand. A valuable resource product that could be mined. He looked around. There were marker pegs staking a mineral claim all over the sandhill. Brady had done a thorough job. He had claimed the mining rights to all this area of Geelup Cove.

The kids were looking at Vim, wondering. Vim's face was so serious and concerned.

Finally Vim stood up.

'Well,' he said, 'if this is what I think it is, Brady is going to come into a lot of money. Yes. A lot of money.'

'Why?' said the kids, puzzled.

'What is it, Vim?' said Kate.

Vim sifted some of the sand through his fingers.

'I think this black stuff is ilmenite. A beach sand, very valuable – it's almost like having your own goldmine, if you own the land where it's found.'

Paul stared at Vim. He didn't understand the full implications, but a number of things about Brady were falling into place. Brady and his strange little bags of sand. Brady in the car park, a little merry. Brady had been celebrating. Celebrating his find. But what did that mean?

'What would happen if you're right and this sand is valuable?' said Paul.

Vim waved, indicating the sandhills and the beach.

'Well – there'd probably be an opencast mine here.'

'What!' said Paul.

'Like a big hole?' said Kate.

'A bit like that, I think,' said Vim.

'But we don't want anything like that in Geelup Cove. It would spoil it!' said Kate.

'No!' said the boys.

They couldn't believe that this beautiful, special part of the island should be destroyed.

Vim's feelings of alarm were the same, but he felt that

he must be cautious. In fact he knew more – he knew that a mine, no matter how carefully it was planned, would bring more people to the island, more houses, more roads, building, development – change. But all the same he felt that he mustn't encourage the kids' reactions. His speculations might be wrong, even if Brady had gone to the trouble to peg his land and to take out a mineral claim.

'Look, I mightn't be right,' he said. 'I'm not really sure that this is ilmenite.'

'How can we tell?' the kids said.

'I think we should take some samples, and then I'll take them to the mainland tomorrow and get them properly analysed.'

'O.K. Then let's do that,' said the kids.

Paul, Kate, Jock and Vim hurried back to the beach and rowed out to the *Isabella*. They got several marine specimen jars from Vim's equipment cupboard, then they went back to the sandhills, and in various places, just as Brady had done, they collected samples of sand.

They soon filled the jars, and Paul filled an empty tin for his own interest. Back on the *Isabella* Vim sealed the jars carefully.

'We'll get an idea of what's going on when I get a report on these tomorrow.'

They spent the rest of the afternoon swimming and playing about in the water with Kate.

As they left Vim that afternoon, Vim said,

'Brady's sand patch is probably nothing to worry about. Even if it is ilmenite it needn't necessarily be a big commercial deposit. It's got to be a fair size to be worth mining.'

The kids felt reassured. They didn't want a mine on their island. But what Vim was doing was reassuring himself as much as reassuring the kids. Falcon Island to him had become a haven – a place away from personal failure, relationships that didn't work out, a business that had failed. Falcon Island was apart from the everyday pressures of the twentieth-century world. It had the charm and peace of a more relaxed period in time. And in a private way it had become important to him.

'O.K. – see you tomorrow when you get back,' the kids said.

'See you, kids!' said Vim. Then to Paul he said, 'We'll go diving again soon, right?'

'Yes – sure,' said Paul, his face lighting up in happiness. He and Vim were friends again.

As the kids rode home the island seemed to turn on some special magic. It was much cooler. The late afternoon sun was slanting through the trees, casting dappled shadows across the road. There was now a light breeze. They could hear the various birds – pigeons cooing in the she-oaks, and cheeky willy wagtails darting in front of them along the road just ahead of their wheels. The island was a very special place.

'It can't be true that there'll be a mine on the island,' said Kate. 'Brady couldn't do that.'

Chapter 6

Frank was still playing tennis when the kids arrived back from the jetty. They opened the front gate and wheeled their bikes up the side path. They were still talking about Brady.

'I reckon the sand can't be that special,' said Jock. 'Somebody would have discovered it before. Old Brady's not that smart.'

They went in the back door. Out of curiosity, while Kate and Jock got a cold drink, Paul went to the bookcase and took out an encyclopaedia. He found 'S', then 'sand'. He read down the page.

'Ah – here! Beach sand. Ilmenite and rutile. Ilmenite is a heavy black beach sand. Well, that part's right.'

'What else does it say?' said Jock.

'It's used for the manufacture of paper and paint and is the basis of titanium oxide – a space-age metal,' said Paul. 'That's what they use for the nose cone on space craft.'

'Wow!' said Jock. 'Now I can see why it's valuable.'

'Does it say anything else?' asked Kate.

'Its specific gravity is 2.5,' he read further. 'That's all.' Paul shut the encyclopaedia.

'What does that mean?' asked Kate.

'It's heavier than ordinary sand,' Paul said.

Jock immediately had an idea.

'We can find out if it's heavier than ordinary sand – then that will half prove that it could be ilmenite.'

'How?' said Paul, sceptical.

'Didn't you bring some back in a tin or something?'

'Yes,' said Paul. 'I'm going to show Dad.'

'We can try to check the specific gravity – the way we did in science at school.'

'Yes! Of course!' said Paul. 'We can!'

'What do we have to do?' said Kate.

'We need lots of jars and things like that,' said Paul.

'There are some in the cupboard,' said Kate.

'Well, let's get them out,' said Paul.

Frank had a very enjoyable afternoon playing tennis. There were a number of keen players to make up sets, including Vicki Fitzgerald, Alan who had a fishing boat, Harry, Mrs Pike (who was pretty fast on the court despite her advancing years) and others.

Frank and Mrs Pike had a really hard battle to beat Vicki Fitzgerald and Alan, but the combined weight of years and experience overcame the younger pair after a prolonged rally.

'A good match, Frank,' said Alan, after it was over.

'You put up quite a fight,' said Frank.

'We're all going to the pub now – do you want to come?' asked Alan.

'Better get home to the kids,' said Frank. 'But thanks very much. Next time perhaps.'

Frank drove home in a relaxed and happy frame of mind. The island was a good place to be. As he parked in the drive he could see the kids' bikes and Jock's. So they were back, he thought. He opened the back door, calling to them.

'Hi, kids – had a good day?'

'Hi, Dad!' said Kate.

Then at the kitchen door Frank stopped. He couldn't believe his eyes. The place was in chaos. There seemed to be mud and sand and empty jars everywhere, with the contents – honey, jam and pickles – sitting in messy bowls on the sink, and buckets of water and wet sand and mud everywhere.

'What do you kids think you're doing!' exclaimed Frank. When he had left the place had been neat and tidy; now it looked as if a cyclone had passed through it.

'We're just about to prove something,' said Paul. Kate and Jock nodded. Paul was carefully filtering a muddy sludge through one of their best tea towels.

'I want an explanation – NOW!' said Frank.

The kids looked up in surprise. Suddenly it dawned on them that Frank was far from pleased. They looked around. For the first time they realised what a mess the kitchen was in.

'Oh-h!' said Paul. 'Sorry, Dad! But you see, we're conducting an experiment.'

'Yes,' said Jock. 'We're doing it the right way. We've got other soils to act as controls – and they all settle at different rates.'

'What experiment?' said Frank. His tone indicated that he was very close to giving them a thorough ticking off.

'Well, we're pretty sure. . . .' began Paul.

'We think we've proved, you mean', said Jock, cutting in, 'that old Brady has found a deposit of ilmenite – that's a valuable beach sand,' he exlained, 'in Geelup Cove.'

'Ilmenite – beach sand – in Geelup Cove?' said Frank, a little bewildered.

Then he said slowly, 'I think you had better start at the beginning and tell me what this is all about.'

Paul took a deep breath. There were things that his father would have to know.

'Well, Dad,' he began, 'it was like this. . . .' And then with help from Kate and Jock, Paul began to tell Frank of the sequence of events over the last month.

During the next half hour Frank listened carefully and

thoughtfully to all the things that Paul and Kate and Jock had to say. They told him everything they knew, although they omitted the midnight spying on Brady's house, considering that that was best left unsaid. They fabricated the story a little by saying that Brady had dropped one of the packets of sand out of his canvas bag near the jetty, and they had found it. Frank felt sure that there was more to the story than this, but decided that probing was not going to add much so he continued to listen quietly, asking an occasional question.

'You saw Brady take samples of sand from different places at Geelup Cove?'

'Yes.'

'Anywhere else?'

'No.'

'And he definitely chased you away because he didn't want you to see what he was doing? You weren't giving him cheek or anything?'

'No!' said all three vehemently.

However, after hearing all the story, Frank's comment was much the same as Vim's.

'Even if there is ilmenite on the island there mightn't be enough to interest a mining company. I think we'll just have to wait and see.'

'But what about all those brochures for new cars and boats that old Brady got?' said Jock.

'It still doesn't add up to much,' said Frank. 'I think all we can do is to wait until Vim comes back tomorrow then we'll know if there's anything to worry about. In the meantime,' Frank then looked at the mess in the kitchen, 'You kids have some cleaning up to do.'

But while Frank changed out of his tennis clothes he thought things over. His job with the Council, which included being part-time Warden for all the Crown Reserves, had made him familiar with the entire island. He knew the calm bays on the leeward side, the wilder western coast, the she-oak thickets, the small lakes and swamp land, the sand dunes and the high scrub-covered hills, and in all of that, he never suspected that the island itself held a factor that could lead to change, even destruction. He knew that he couldn't let the matter rest. He needed to know more.

Suddenly he thought – Alf Dixon had lived on the island for thirty years. He might be able to throw some light on the matter. When he went back to the kitchen to check on the clean-up, he said to Jock:

'I'll run you home, Jock. I want to have a word with your Grandpop.'

With the three kids in the cab, and Jock's bike in the back of the truck, Frank drove out of the town along the narrow road that led to Jock's place.

Nan's weekend sign, 'Fruit, Vegetables and Honey for Sale', was still standing near the gate. Nan and Alf were in the back garden watering the flowerbeds.

They were surprised but pleased to see Frank.

'What have the nippers been up to today?' said Alf with a wink at Kate. This was his standard remark when he saw Frank and the kids.

'Nothing that can't be fixed,' said Frank.

'Well, that's something then!' said Jock's Nan, smiling conspiratorially at them. Jock's Nan was a sharp old lady with a good sense of humour. Jock was very like her.

'But cleaning up took quite a while,' said Frank.

'Ah. I see!' said Nan. 'In strife are they? What's the story now?'

'They spread sand right through the house,' said Frank.

'Hold on, Dad,' said Paul. 'Only in the kitchen.'

Nan laughed. 'What next!'

'There was a bit of a mess,' said Frank, 'But in a way that's what I want to see you about, Alf. The kids were experimenting,' said Frank. 'You see, they think that they've found ilmenite on Jack Brady's land.'

'Ilmenite!' Alf whistled. He knew what that might

mean. There'd been quite a lot in the papers about ilmenite deposits in Queensland. There'd been considerable opposition to mining there.

'Has anyone ever said anything about ilmenite on Falcon Island in the past?' asked Frank.

Alf pushed his head back thoughtfully. His weather-beaten face was serious.

'Well, now you mention it,' he said, 'I'd forgotten all about it – but years ago – there was a geologist here – working for a week or so. There was some talk then about finding traces of ilmenite. But nothing ever came of it!'

'I wish we knew more,' said Frank.

'Why don't you go and tackle old Brady?' said Jock.

'No,' said Frank. 'I considered that. But somehow I have a feeling we'd better be careful. I think we must get all our facts straight first.'

'Rats!' said Jock, who was longing for a chance to have a go at Brady. Brady had kept what he had found secret, so he must be up to no good, in Jock's opinion.

Nan seemed to have the same attitude.

'You'll have to watch Jack Brady – he's as cunning as a sack of monkeys.'

'Trust the kids to find out,' said Alf with a laugh. Then he became serious again.

'There could be quite a problem, you know,' he said. 'If there is ilmenite here, Jack Brady could carve up the whole place.'

'Well, he's pegged out his own block, I gather,' said Frank. 'He's secured the rights to the sand there.'

Alf shook his head.

'It could be a bad business. But I tell you what – if he thinks he's going to turn Falcon Island into a mine, he'll have a fight on his hands.'

'Good on you, Mr Dixon,' said Kate.

'Let's hope there's nothing to it,' said Nan. But her

tone wasn't convincing. Nan and Alf, Frank and the kids all knew that there could be quite a serious situation to face, something much bigger than ordinary everyday affairs. They had a shared sense of anxiety – there could be problems ahead for Falcon Island.

After school the next day Kate and Jock and Paul went down to the jetty straight away, hoping that Vim might be back from having the sand samples tested.

'Not here yet,' said Paul as they reached the jetty.

They sat waiting, watching jellyfish float between the jetty piles.

Up in the town Frank and Alf were also waiting for Vim's return. They'd decided to replace some kerbing, so that they would be working close by, to be on hand when Vim returned.

On the jetty the kids had each selected a jellyfish and were having a jellyfish race, timed by Jock. Their chosen jellyfish had to pass a certain part of the jetty by a given time. But the jellyfish, not knowing about the race, were uncooperative, and went wafting in all directions concerned with their own business.

Then Kate sighed.

'Gosh – I wish Vim would come back. I wonder what he's found out. It'd be awful if anything happened to Falcon Island.'

Then Jock gave a shout. In the far distance he saw the *Isabella* approaching the island.

'It's Vim!'

The kids stood and watched as the *Isabella* approached. Vim brought his boat smoothly into the mooring. Paul caught the line.

'What's the result?' called Jock.

Vim jumped on to the jetty.

'Sorry, kids,' he said. 'It's ilmenite all right – and they think it could have good commercial possibilities!'

'Oh!' said Paul, disappointed. He had been hoping that the scientific test would prove that their experiments were wrong. 'Well,' he said, 'I expect we'd better tell Dad.'

Together Vim, Paul, Jock and Kate went up to the town. They found Frank and Alf outside the Post Office, finishing up for the day. Frank could tell at once by the expression on their faces what the result was.

'Not good news?' Frank said.

'I finally got to the right department after a hassle,' Vim said. 'They confirmed it. It's ilmenite and it'd be worth mining if the deposit is big enough.'

'Brady took a couple of dozen samples from all over his property, so the kids say,' said Frank. Paul nodded. 'And he came back like a man who'd just found out that his backyard was full of gold nuggets.'

'If he can lease his property to a mining company for the right price, that's just as good,' said Alf.

'But we don't want a mine on Falcon Island,' protested Kate.

'I think it's about time we asked Jack Brady a few questions,' said Frank grimly.

'Well, you don't have to go far, Dad,' said Paul. He pointed. Brady had just come out of the side door of the pub, carrying several crates of empty bottles.

'Hey – Jack!' called Frank. 'Could I have a word with you?'

Brady reacted with surprise. He dumped the crates on the back of his truck.

'Yeah – what is it?' he said.

Frank and Alf, with the kids and Vim, crossed the road.

Inside the Post Office, Mrs Yates had noticed the group of Frank and the others, and as she had expected that at any moment one of them would come into the store, she had been keeping a close watch. To her surprise, Frank had hailed Brady. And the tone of his voice was abrupt, which wasn't like Frank. Intrigued, Mrs Yates moved closer to the window.

Beside his truck, Brady was impatient.

'What do you want?' he said to Frank.

'It's probably nothing much, said Frank, 'but I wanted to ask you about something that's been worrying Alf and me.'

'Well, what is it?' said Brady, even more impatient.

'To get right to the point,' said Frank, 'it's the question of mining ilmenite.'

Brady looked as if he'd been hit by a ten-tonne truck. His jaw dropped.

'What!' He was so flabbergasted he was virtually speechless. His reaction told Frank and Alf and Vim and the kids all they needed to know.

Inside the Post Office, Mrs Yates had put her head out of the door to see what was going on. There seemed to be some sort of trouble brewing. But she couldn't hear.

Frank asked again. 'Is there ilmenite on your property? And more to the point, what are you going to do about it?'

Brady had managed to recover. 'Mind your own business!' he said.

'If there are plans to mine sand on Falcon Island,' said Alf, becoming heated, 'it *is* my business. It's everyone's business.'

Mrs Yates's curiosity had grown to the point where she had left the Post Office and had joined Vim and the kids.

'What's going on?' she whispered to Paul.

'Could be a mine on Falcon Island,' said Paul in an undertone.

'Oh,' she said, not really following, but thinking that Paul was referring to an explosive mine; occasionally a few from the War appeared on the beaches. She was very perturbed.

'Something must be done about it,' she said.

Brady looked as if he was going to get into his truck to drive off. But Frank stepped forward a little, to block him.

'Well?' said Frank. 'What's the answer?'

Brady paused. Then, belligerently, he said, 'I told you to mind your own bloody business. What I do with my property is my business.'

'Oh my goodness!' said Mrs Yates.

Brady noticed Mrs Yates for the first time.

'What's she doing here?' he said to Frank.

Mrs Yates was furious.

'And who are you speaking of – the cat's mother?' she said.

Brady just looked at her.

'I don't know what you intend to mine, but I'll tell you this, Jack Brady,' said Mrs Yates, 'nobody, I repeat, nobody is going to interfere with anything on Falcon Island. It is all part of our irreplaceable heritage.'

'That's right,' said Alf warmly.

'Good on you, Mrs Yates,' said Jock.

Brady glared at them. 'You're hopeless, the lot of you,' he said. 'This place is just about dead. It needs something to bring it back to life, it needs stirring up before it gives up the ghost.'

'I think I'll get the Constable,' said Mrs Yates, convinced that Brady intended to blow up the island.

'What the heck is she on about?' said Brady to Frank. 'You ought to put a muzzle on her.'

'Hold on a minute, Jack,' said Frank, who could see that Mrs Yates was getting into a state. But Mrs Yates was quite capable of defending herself.

'You've no right to talk to me like that, Jack Brady,' she said dramatically. 'Your behaviour is a disgrace to anyone who has any feeling. And if you go ahead with mining anything, it will be over my dead body.' With that she looked as if she were about to launch herself like a juggernaut upon Brady, who was only half her size. There was a round of applause from Alf and the kids.

'Just a minute, Dorothy,' said Frank, grabbing her arm.

'What is she talking about? She's off her head,' said Brady, retreating in alarm.

'Just give us an answer,' said Frank.

There seemed to be no escape for Brady.

'Well – you can like it or lump it,' he said. 'The Barron-West Sand Mining Company will be here to negotiate with me within the next few days. And that's that.'

Brady left his truck and stalked back to the hotel.

'For heaven's sake!' said Mrs Yates, a bit shaky.

'You spoke up very well, Mrs Yates,' said Paul.

'You were terrific!' said Kate.

'But what I don't understand is why he wants to blow up half the island,' said Mrs Yates, now a little tearful.

Paul caught on faster than the others.

'Not a *land* mine, Mrs Yates! A *sand* mine. Mr Brady wants to mine the beach sands.'

Confusion crossed Mrs Yates's face. But then she understood.

'That's the most outrageous thing I've heard of!' she said. 'A sand mine on Falcon Island? Never!'

'We're inclined to think much the same,' said Frank.

'Yes,' said Alf. 'Brady's land comes close to the town. It could ruin the place! But I tell you what – there'll be quite a few people on Falcon Island who will agree with Jack Brady. Just you wait and see. I reckon the island is in for trouble.'

'We will have to see what we can do to stop him,' said Mrs Yates.

Frank was in complete agreement. He glanced at his watch.

'I think I'll ring this sand mining company,' said Frank. 'It isn't five o'clock yet. Brady could be all talk. I'd like to know something definite.

'Yes,' said Alf.

'It was the Barron-West Company,' said Paul.

'Use the Post Office telephone,' said Mrs Yates, who didn't want to miss anything.

'I think I'll be off now,' said Vim quietly.

It seemed that no one heard him. But Paul did.

'See you, Vim.'

As Vim walked back to his boat he felt a sense of unease and unhappiness. Was there no way of avoiding pressures and problems? There seemed to be no escape from then. Why did the outside world have to invade the island? Why couldn't it remain lost in time? Vim was still in the same mood when he set out to check his bait traps. He knew that he had some thinking to do.

In the Post Office Frank, with Alf and the kids and Mrs Yates crowding around, had got hold of a Mr Bob Scott, who was a senior executive of the Barron-West Sand Mining firm. Frank was surprised to find that Mr Scott spoke very courteously, and that he seemed anxious to be cooperative.

'I understand that your firm is interested in a sand mine proposal on Falcon Island,' Frank said.

'Yes,' said Mr Scott. 'There is a proposal to that effect.'

'How definite is it?' asked Frank.

There was a slight pause at the other end. Mr Scott was apparently taken aback by Frank's bluntness, but nevertheless he answered politely, 'We've taken an option for three months.'

'We're a bit concerned about it over here,' said Frank.

'Oh?' said Mr Scott. 'In what way? I understood that the entire island was behind the project.'

'Typical of Jack Brady!' said Frank. Trust Jack to put that sort of story over, he thought.

'What!' said Mr Scott in alarm on the other end of the telephone. 'I understood there were no objections.'

'The islanders should have been informed,' said Frank.

'Oh – I see,' said Mr Scott. 'Naturally I assumed that everyone knew that there was a proposal being considered. Of course we have to make a thorough feasibility study, so nothing's finalised yet – but the assay samples look very encouraging from our point of view.'

'So you mean that you will be going ahead?'

'It's still an option situation, Mr Ellery,' said Mr Scott. 'And we may not proceed. Although . . . it's very likely that we will.'

'Can't you give a definite answer?' said Frank.

'It's all that I can say at the moment,' said Mr Scott. 'But keep in touch.'

'Thanks very much, Mr Scott,' said Frank, and hung up.

'Well . . .?' said Kate and Mrs Yates together.

'He seemed quite a nice bloke,' said Frank.

'But what about the sand mine?' said Kate.

'He hedged a bit – but I reckon he's really interested,' said Frank.

'What are we going to do?' said Mrs Yates.

'We'll have to have a community meeting to discuss the issue,' said Frank.

Chapter 7

That evening a hastily called meeting of the Falcon Island Community Association was held in the school.

Frank outlined to the Committee the information that he had so far, and added, 'I feel that everyone on the island should be informed and have the opportunity to voice their opinion.'

'We should send out notices,' said Nan.

Miss Fitzgerald said, 'I'll do them on the school duplicator and the children can deliver them.'

'We'd better get an agenda ready,' said Frank.

'One of the things that concerns me most,' said Miss Fitzgerald, 'the sand mining company would undoubtedly be carting sand in trucks. But which road would they use? I think they'd probably have to pass the school.'

'If they were taking it to be loaded at the jetty, that's exactly what would happen,' said Frank.

'We must prevent that,' said Mrs Yates.

'I move that we get an authority over here to tell us exactly what will be involved in this sand mining,' said Alf. 'He can be guest speaker at the meeting.'

'I second that,' said Nan.

'I've got a mate who could put me on to somebody,' said Frank.

'Right, Frank, you arrange it for next Saturday,' said Alf.

The next day at the school, Miss Fitzgerald organised the notices and asked who would be prepared to deliver them. Kate and Jock and Paul had already told all the children at the school about Jack Brady's proposed sand mine. Every single one of them opposed the idea, so there was no lack of willing volunteers to deliver the notices.

The children who lived around the old fish canning factory took notices for their part of the island, the children who lived near the golf course took notices for the people who lived there, and Kate and Wendy and Jock and Paul undertook to deliver notices around the town.

As soon as school was out, Kate and Wendy went in one direction and Jock and Paul went in the other.

The response of most of the islanders was amazement that such an important thing as a potential new industry on the island had got so far without anyone knowing anything about it.

'Jack Brady keeps his cards close to his chest, that's for sure,' said Herb, chuckling, as he leant on his rake in his garden.

'You will come?' said Kate.

'I'll be there,' said Herb.

'Eleven o'clock sharp,' said Kate.

The boys found that delivering the notices was very straightforward except for Mr Meredith, who mistook them for religious callers and slammed the door in their faces.

After an hour or so, the boys found that they still had several notices left.

'Let's take one to Vim,' said Jock.

The boys rode down towards the jetty. They found Vim cleaning down the deck of the *Isabella*. He took the notice and put it in his hip pocket.

'You will come?' asked Paul.

'Maybe,' said Vim.

Paul was startled. 'I thought you would be there. . . .' he began.

'I was planning to dive on Saturday morning, before

the breeze comes in. The water gets a bit choppy now that it's almost the end of summer.'

'But you've got to come!' insisted Jock.

'I will if I can,' said Vim. He was smiling, but he obviously wasn't going to commit himself. Paul felt disappointed, but then Vim said,

'I'm thinking of tackling Dutchman's Bay.'

'Gee! Super!' said Jock. 'You'll be diving into the caverns?'

'That's right,' said Vim. 'I was going to ask if you wanted to come with me,' he added.

'After the meeting we could,' said Paul. He looked at Jock. He could see that Jock was very keen to go with Vim.

'We have to go to the meeting first,' Paul said.

Jock, although a bit disappointed, agreed.

'Yes, we'll have to go to the meeting.'

'O.K.,' Vim said. 'What about Sunday?'

'That'd be fine,' said Paul.

'Great!' said Jock.

'Check with your Dad and Grandpop first,' said Vim. 'It's a bit rougher out there.'

'We will. See you then, Vim,' said the boys.

As they left the jetty Paul felt strangely disappointed. He'd badly wanted Vim to say that he would come to the meeting, ready to fight with them against the sand mining issue. But it seemed as if Vim was avoiding the situation, as if he didn't want to be involved. And yet Vim was their friend. Paul didn't understand Vim's attitude at all. He was still feeling unhappy when they got to their bikes.

'Gee – I'm hot,' said Jock. 'Why don't we go for a swim? And we can deliver notices to the people in the fishing shacks at the same time.'

'O.K.,' said Paul.

The boys got on their bikes and rode through the town and out on the road to Geelup Cove. They quickly took the detour off the road to Wireless Hill and delivered the remainder of the notices to the few families in the holiday fishing shacks, and then rode out towards Geelup Cove.

Jock was leading as they came over the crest of the hill that led to Geelup Cove. He came to a sudden stop.

'Hey – Paul! Our track to the beach has been fenced off!'

Sure enough, between stakes flying fluttering orange ribbons, there was a fence – of sorts. It had been constructed from old sheets of corrugated iron and rolls of rusty barbed wire, and there was a prominent notice, 'Trespassers Will Be Prosecuted', nailed on a post.

'What a nerve!' said Paul. 'What a rotten thing to do.'

They rode up to look at it.

'Well,' said Jock, 'old Brady's found some use for his junk at last!'

'It looks like a prisoner of war camp,' said Paul.

'It doesn't do much to add to the appearance of the island, does it?' said Jock bitterly.

'Well, there's no point in staying here,' said Paul. 'We might as well go home.'

Jock was examining a way of getting through the fence.

'Forget it, Jock,' said Paul. 'If Brady found us on his property he'd go to Dad and there'd be a fight. I know Dad wants to keep things really cool until after everyone has had a chance to talk about Brady's land at the meeting.

'Damn,' said Jock. 'Now what will we do?'

'There's nothing we can do.'

'Well – why don't we go and swim in Settlement Bay?' said Jock.

'I want to go home,' said Paul.

It was a very dispirited Paul who left Jock after their hot ride back. Suddenly everything on the island seemed to have gone wrong, especially his friendship with Vim. When he met up with Kate she said, 'Golly, Paulie – what's the matter!'

He told her about Brady's fence, but not about Vim.

'Brady can't do that!' exclaimed Kate.

'He's quite within his rights,' said Paul.

Kate felt very upset. 'Can't we stop people from doing things we don't like?' she said.

'That's what Dad hopes the meeting will decide,' said Paul. 'We'll just have to wait and see.'

In some strange way, for Jock, Paul and Kate the next few days were the flattest and dullest they could remember for ages. There seemed to be nothing to do. And they began to feel pushed aside. The adults were taking over the sand mining issue – it was growing beyond their initial discovery.

As for Brady, he was nowhere to be seen, and neither was Vim for that matter.

From his desk at school Paul could see the *Isabella* in her mooring pen, but by afternoon she had gone. They couldn't swim at Geelup Cove, and when they went to swim in Settlement Bay it was full of seaweed and jellyfish. Nothing was right.

It was in a completely negative mood that Paul refused to go to the store on Friday afternoon to pick up the vegetables and milk. He made Kate go instead.

'Lazy thing!' Kate said as she rode off indignantly.

But at the Post Office Store Kate was rewarded by a warm welcome from Mrs Yates.

'It *is* nice to see you, Katey,' she said.

'I've come for the stores,' said Kate.

'Now what was it?' said Mrs Yates.

'Lettuce, bananas. . . .' began Kate.

At that moment the squeaky door to the Post Office Store opened. It was Jack Brady.

'Hullo, Mr Brady!' said Kate. She thought she ought to be polite.

'Humph!' said Jack Brady. Kids again. They were always under your feet.

'Come for your mail, have you?' said Mrs Yates sweetly.

'Yes,' growled Brady.

'There's quite a bit,' said Mrs Yates, turning to the pigeonhole where the letters were held. 'You haven't been in for a few days.'

Brady gave another inaudible growl in reply.

Mrs Yates handed the mail over. Brady took it and was about to leave.

'Oh – Mr Brady,' said Mrs Yates.

'What?' said Brady, impatiently, near the door.

Mrs Yates had a crafty little smile on her face. To Kate she looked like a purring tabby cat, about to pounce.

'There's a notice in that mail,' she said.

'Oh yeah?' said Brady as if he couldn't be bothered wasting his time.

'It concerns you,' said Mrs Yates as if she were about to pat him with a sheathed claw.

'Yeah?' said Brady. He looked very suspicious.

He sorted through the mail. He put the letters in his shirt pocket, retaining a sheet of paper which Kate recognised as one of the notices she had been delivering.

'You ought to read it,' said Mrs Yates.

Brady unfolded the notice; slowly his eyes travelled down. 'A meeting will be held,' he said, reading aloud. 'So what?' he said. 'No meeting's going to put me off.'

But then he got to the bit that Kate knew read, 'An expert conservationist, Mr John Carter, will be invited to address the meeting about the consequences sand mining could have on our island and environment'.

Brady's face went from a dark sort of red to purple.

'Hell! A conservationist!' he said. 'Tomorrow!'

He stood staring at the notice as if stunned.

'That's right,' said Mrs Yates, with a small smile of satisfaction.

'Interfering old so and so!' he said in fury.

Mrs Yates merely smiled. Kate could see that she didn't care what Brady called her. She was having the greatest pleasure in seeing his arrogance deflated.

'The whole community is going to fight you, Jack Brady,' said Mrs Yates. But Brady hadn't stopped to hear. He had bolted out of the door.

Mrs Yates's smile was as if she had just had a bowl of cream.

'That's fixed him!' she said.

Outside, Brady had made a dive for the phone box. His shaking hand could scarcely dial the number he wanted. The phone seemed to take forever to be answered. He'd just managed to get through and start speaking when Kate came out of the shop.

'Is that you, mate?' said Brady, quite clearly.

In his agitation Brady was speaking so loudly that Kate was aware of everything he was saying as she put the stores in the carrier of her bicycle. She became interested. She thought she'd wait to hear some more.

'I tell you there's real trouble,' Brady went on urgently. 'The locals are getting a conservationist. . . .'

Kate waited, fiddling with the chain on her bicycle.

'Yes – that's right!' said Brady. Then he said, '. . . will you come over tomorrow night? Right. Wireless Hill. Good. Twelve o'clock – be seeing you!' Brady hung up.

Kate, still beside her bike, became a bit nervous. Would Brady see her? But her fears weren't realised. Brady left the phone box seemingly almost stupefied and, without a backward glance, crossed the road towards the garage where his truck was parked.

The notice really got old Brady stirred up, Kate thought. Serves him right. With some glee she grabbed her bike to set off to find Paul and tell him.

Brady's emotions were quite different from Kate's. As he crossed the road he was in a state of combined bewilderment and shock. An interfering conservationist at the island meeting! The opposition really meant to get him – that was certain. The meddling fools! What right had they to get involved in his business? In Brady's mind there were no issues to discuss. He'd taken all the proper steps. He'd discovered the ilmenite, and he'd pegged his claim. That had cost him a few quid. Then he'd had to get a lawyer to tell him what he was entitled to, before he had discussions with the Barron-West Sand Mining Company. That had been more expense. But he'd done it all the right way. He was completely within his rights, and if everything worked out the royalties paid by the sand mining company would set him up for the rest of his life.

By the time he had reached his truck, although he was still appalled, his first shock was starting to recede. His anger was building up. He was beginning to think. He wasn't going to let them get away with it! He'd think of something, some way of fixing them – somehow.

When Kate got home, Jock was in the kitchen with Paul. She could hardly wait to tell them.

'Hey! You won't believe it!' she said. 'Mrs Yates gave Brady one of those notices about the meeting!'

'Gee – she was game!' said Jock.

'What did he say?' said Paul.

'He didn't say much – he just rushed out to the phone box.' Kate started to giggle. 'He was really furious.

'Didn't he say anything at all?' said Paul.

'He didn't to Mrs Yates, but on the phone he did. You should have seen him – he was really furious. He said there was a lot of trouble here!' She laughed. And then she added, puzzled, 'What I don't understand is why he wants to meet this person on the beach. At night. Why not on the jetty? It's daft.'

'Say that again,' said Jock, instantly alert. 'What is he going to do?'

'Brady's going to meet someone on the beach – tonight.'

'Did he say why?'

'No,' said Kate. 'He was really angry – that's all.'

Jock whistled. 'Why on the beach and not on the jetty?'

'That's what I was wondering too,' said Paul.

'Maybe he doesn't want anyone to see him,' said Kate.

'That's just what occurred to me!' said Jock. 'Did he say what time?' The boys were taking Brady's reaction to the notice of the meeting more seriously than Kate had.

'About midnight – or something,' she said. 'Why do you want to know?'

'I think we should go and see what Brady's up to,' said Jock.

'And that's what I think too,' said Paul.

Creeping out to check up on Brady on this occasion was much more difficult than the first time. It was so late when the alarm went off. Paul lay in bed not wanting to get up. But he forced himself out of bed. Rousing Kate was difficult. Then they had to tiptoe cautiously through the house. Frank, however, was oblivious to what his children were doing. He was sound asleep.

Kate and Paul ran all the way through the darkness to meet Jock, but when they got to their meeting place, Jock wasn't there.

'Blow!' said Paul. 'We'll have to wait for him.'

'I hope he won't be long,' said Kate.

Suddenly in the bush nearby there was a long mournful sigh, followed by a plaintive sobbing sound.

'What's that?' said Kate, jumping in fright.

The mournful sound was repeated, a whimpering moan.

'Crumbs, what it is?' said Kate, really scared.

Paul knew what it was.

'Cut it out, Jock!' he said furiously.

There was a rustle in the bushes, then silence.

'Come on, Jock!' said Paul.

Jock emerged from the bushes.

'Don't you think my ghostly rattle was super?' he said.

'No,' said Paul.

'Golly – look at you!' said Kate.

Now that he was out of shadow, they could see him. He did look spectacular. He was all in black again, but with a difference. He had a black stocking pulled down over his head, making his face look like a flat squashed bug.

'Yuk!' said Kate.

'Nan's,' mumbled Jock. He put his hand in a pocket.

'I've got one for each of you too,' he said.

Paul was unimpressed.

'We don't need anything like that,' he said.

Jock pulled his stocking back so that he could speak more readily.

'Go on,' he said. 'You ought to cover up your blonde hair.'

'No,' said Paul. He looked at his watch. It was twenty to twelve.

'You've got no idea how to do things,' said Jock, hurt.

'No time,' said Paul, already off, and running down the road in the direction of Wireless Hill.

Kate and Jock had to sprint to catch up with Paul. He kept up a fast pace. By the time they had reached the climb that led up to Wireless Hill, they were puffed and beginning to slow down.

Then from behind they heard the engine of an approaching vehicle.

'Quick! Hide!' said Paul.

As Kate, Paul and Jock dived into the bushes on the side of the road, a truck came round the bend, headlights blinding. It roared up and over the hill.

'Brady,' said Paul. He glanced at the luminous dial of his watch. 'And he's right on time. We'd better move.'

Paul led Kate and Jock up the hill, making them run in the soft sand at the side of the road to muffle their footsteps. When they reached the crest they could see that Brady had turned and parked. He was just getting out of his truck, carrying a large torch – a storm lantern used on fishing boats at night.

Paul motioned Jock and Kate to hide behind some boulders. As a seemingly endless procession of clouds passed across the sky and the pale moonlight was reflected up from the white sand, the effect was strangely creepy. The wind lifted and sent a small breeze through the dune grass, making it move mysteriously. Kate felt nervous, but both the boys were intent. Jock and Paul were watching everything that Brady did.

Brady now began to make his way down the path towards the beach. The powerful light from his torch threw a pool of light. It bobbed along for a short distance as Brady negotiated the top part of the path. Then it disappeared. Brady was now out of sight.

'O.K. – let's go down as well,' said Paul. He had taken command again. He signalled that Kate and Jock were to move forward.

They ran swiftly over the open space that lay between where they were hiding and the top of the path. Once they reached the path they had to move very cautiously. It was steep and difficult to negotiate without a torch. Paul went first, then Kate, then Jock. They crept down until they came to a bend in the path. Then they could see the indistinct shape of Brady below, and the yellow splash of light from his storm lantern.

'Ssh! Wait!' whispered Paul. They watched. Brady had now reached the beach. He turned off his torch. Then within a few seconds he had turned it on again. Then it was off, then he switched it on again, in a regular pattern.

'What's he doing?' whispered Kate.

'He's signalling, I think,' said Paul.

Then out on the water, in the darkness of the sea, there was an answering flash of light, which flickered off and then on in reply. Paul's supposition was answered.

As they watched Brady kept up his signalling as the

boat came closer and closer. The kids could now hear the purr of a small outboard motor.

'It's coming in,' said Jock, in an undertone.

With his storm lantern still on, Brady crossed the beach.

'Quick! We'll have to hide,' said Paul. He led Kate and Jock down from their exposed position to a clump of rock at the bottom of the path where they could safely hide and not be seen.

'There's the boat,' whispered Jock.

They could make out the shape of a small rubber dinghy, now in shallow water. Brady turned out the storm lantern and waded into the sea to help pull the boat in. The kids could vaguely distinguish the bulky outline of a man in a waterproof jacket, as he got out of the rubber dinghy.

There were muffled voices. Brady, on the beach, greeted his mate with a sense of relief.

'Mike – glad you could get over here!' he said.

'It was a bit tricky bringing her in the dark. Got a bit damp,' the large man replied.

'Well, then, don't let's hang about,' said Brady.

Together they pulled the rubber dinghy on to the beach, carried it up beyond the high water mark and put it behind some protecting rocks. Then Brady got his storm lantern.

'Right, Mike! Back to my place.'

'What are they saying?' whispered Kate.

'Can't hear anything,' said Paul. The sound of the sea lapping against the nearby flat rocks drowned their voices.

'Here they come!' said Jock.

The kids crouched further back into the dark protection of the rock clump at the base of the path. They were continuing to strain to hear what Brady was saying.

'It's easier at high tide,' said Brady, as the two men approached.

'A bit rough in the channel,' said the man beside him. His voice was muffled. All the kids could see was that he carried a small overnight bag. The light from Brady's storm lantern now appeared dangerously close, and his boots seemed to be within a hair's-breadth of Paul's face. Surely he must see us, Paul thought, his heart beating hard, but they walked on.

'That's because there's been an easterly,' said Brady.

'Yeah, I reckon,' said Brady's mate. Then he coughed. It was a harsh, tight cough, as if he had an irritation deep in his chest.

'You can change your gear when we get to my place,' said Brady. Then they went on up the path, the light from the torch disappearing, and the sound of their footsteps, as they negotiated the rocks, fading.

Jock was the first to speak.

'I don't believe it!' he said. 'We've come all this way only to hear old Brady mumbling on and offering his mate a dry pair of jeans!'

He was completely disgusted.

Paul was very disappointed. The whole thing had been a failure. They had found out nothing.

'It was a real flop,' he said. 'We might as well go home.'

Above, they heard Brady's truck drive off.

They started to stumble up the hill. They were all very tired.

'I'm exhausted,' yawned Kate.

'What a disaster!' said Paul.

'Gee – the things Brady does don't make sense,' said Jock.

As they wearily headed for the road, it seemed an impossibly long way home, and the road stony and rough. They felt totally exhausted and deflated as they stumbled towards the sleeping township.

Chapter 8

Back at his house, Brady put the kettle on while Mike Jarvis went to change into some dry clothes. He got out two battered cups and two equally battered mismatching saucers from the cupboard, and the milk from his ancient refrigerator.

As Mike Jarvis came back into the room, Brady quickly cleared a space by shoving aside some newspapers and dirty socks.

'Sit here, mate,' he said, pointing to the only comfortable chair.

'Thanks,' said Jarvis.

'Want a cuppa?'

'Yeah – too right.' Jarvis started to cough. 'Might warm me up.'

While Mike Jarvis settled himself into the chair, Brady fumbled around getting things ready. He wasn't used to having visitors.

'Won't be long,' said Brady.

'That's all right,' said Jarvis, still choking. 'This cough – it gets me every now and then.'

The kettle began to whistle. Brady made the tea. He was about to pour milk into the cup when he said, 'Like a nip in it instead of milk?' reaching for a bottle of brandy on the shelf above him. Jarvis, still trying to cope with the tickle in his chest, nodded.

Brady poured some brandy into the black tea, vigorously stirred in a teaspoonful of sugar and handed it to his mate.

'That'll fix ya.'

Jarvis drank half the cup and gave a pleasurable sigh. 'Ah! That's getting to the right place,' he said.

Feeling warmer he leant back in the chair as Brady refilled the cup and added another dash of brandy.

'Now, Jack,' said Jarvis, 'Give us the details.'

Brady immediately scowled.

'Well, it's about the option to mine sand on my property. . . .'

'Yeah? What about it?' Jarvis, who dealt in Brady's illegal crayfishing, knew all about Brady's discovery of ilmenite on his formerly worthless sand block of land.

'Well, what's happened', said Brady, 'is that the locals over here have invited a conservationist to talk to the meeting tomorrow.'

A grave sense of injustice arose in Brady again.

'You know what these idiots here are like – they'll believe anything they're told, and a conservationist would tell them that sand mining would ruin the place, and then they'll kick up a fuss and the sand mining company will pull out.'

'You could be right,' said Jarvis. 'It has happened before.'

'Yeah, I know,' said Brady. 'Anyway, after a bit I thought – two can play at that game! I want to muddy the waters a bit.' He smiled at the thought.

'Yeah . . . yeah – but where do I come in?' said Jarvis.

'I want you to put my side of it. All the advantages and that. Tell 'em how good it'll be for the island – that sort of thing.'

'Well, I don't mind helping you out, mate,' said Jarvis, 'but that could be a bit tricky.'

'No. I've got it all worked out,' said Brady with a rare chuckle. A gleam of mirth twinkled in his eyes. 'It'll begin with a little case of hijacking.'

'What?' said Jarvis, startled.

'It's simple,' said Brady.

Then, lowering his voice conspiratorially, he gave Jarvis the details of his plan.

At a quarter to ten the next morning, the kids still hadn't come to have their breakfast. Frank went to the bedroom door.

'Hey, kids!' he said. 'Come on! Wake up.'

Paul and Kate both opened their eyes with great reluctance.

'Come on, zombies!' said Frank.

The lure of cooking bacon finally made Kate and Paul crawl out of bed. They felt terrible. They sat at the kitchen table, bleary-eyed and yawning.

'What's the matter with you two?' Frank said, giving them their breakfast. 'You're not getting sick, are you?'

'No. We're all right.'

Frank looked at them anxiously.

'Maybe a dose of tonic is called for,' he said.

'No!' protested Kate, who hated the black bitter stuff that Frank dosed them with from time to time.

However, Frank's intention to get the tonic bottle was interrupted by a discreet knock at the back door.

'Come in,' called Frank.

There was a tap again. Surprised, because people didn't stand on ceremony on Falcon Island, Frank went to the door and opened it. On the doorstep stood a stranger, a tall, very well dressed, distinguished-looking bald-headed man, his face beaming with a friendly and engaging smile.

'Frank Ellery?'

'Yes,' said Frank, a little surprised.

'I'm John Carter,' said Mike Jarvis, now in the role that Brady had prepared for him – an impersonation of the conservationist expected by the Falcon Island Community Association.

'Oh – Mr Carter,' said Frank, a little taken aback because he wasn't quite ready.

'I'm pleased to meet you,' said Mike Jarvis as they shook hands.

'Come in,' said Frank. He brought Mike Jarvis into the kitchen.

'I didn't expect you so soon,' said Frank. 'I was going to meet the ferry – is it in already?'

Frank glanced at the clock. It was only a quarter past ten.

'A friend came over for a fishing trip. I got a ride,' said Jarvis smoothly.

'Well – anyway, I'm glad you could accept our invitation. We didn't give you much notice.' Frank's smile was warm and welcoming. Then he remembered Kate and Paul sitting at the table.

'Oh – and these are my kids, Kate and Paul,' he said, indicating the children.

'Hi, kids!' said Mike Jarvis.

'Hullo, Mr Carter.'

Frank was still a little at a loss that the conservationist should have turned up so early. He said:

'Look, give me a minute or two to get changed and I'll take you to meet some of the committee members, then we can fill you in on what's happened so far.'

'Fine,' said Mike Jarvis.

'Make Mr Carter some coffee,' Frank said to Paul.

'No – don't bother,' said Mike Jarvis. 'I'll just sit here and wait.'

'I won't be long,' said Frank.

As Frank left, Mike Jarvis sat on the edge of the table. The kids looked at one another. They didn't know what to say. Mike Jarvis kept smiling at them but he didn't say anything. An awkward silence developed. Finally Paul felt that he had to break the deadlock.

'It's really good of you to come over, Mr Carter,' he said politely.

'I hope people get really mad and stop the sand mining,' said Kate.

'Yes. Er – yes,' said Mike Jarvis.

There was another silence.

'Do you work as a conservationist all the time?' said Kate.

There was a slight pause. 'Well, I'm a marine biologist actually,' said Mike Jarvis. He and Brady had decided that this was the best answer to give. After all, as a dealer in Marine spare parts and Brady's mate in black market crayfish, he knew a bit about maritime matters.

Kate's face lit up.

'Gee – that's super!' she said. 'Paul knows a lot about sea birds and the reefs and things like that.'

'That's very nice,' said Mike Jarvis heartily, but suddenly feeling a little uncomfortable.

Paul saw an opportunity to ask a question that concerned him.

'Do you think they'll ever find out what happens to crayfish in its larval stage?' he said.

Jarvis felt a little disconcerted for a moment, but decided that he must bluff his way through.

'I'm sure we will,' he said with authority. 'We'll follow its movements on the reefs and watch it change from egg to larva to immature crayfish.'

Paul was puzzled. This Mr Carter who said he was a marine biologist! What was he saying? Didn't he know that crayfish larva weren't found on the reefs? But before Paul could ask another question Frank, now changed and dressed in his best slacks and shirt, appeared.

'Right,' said Frank. 'We're not here. See you kids at the meeting.'

'See you, kids!' said Mike Jarvis.

Frank led Mike Jarvis out of the kitchen.

'Gee – that bloke's a funny guy,' said Paul.

'What's the matter?' said Kate.

'I don't think he knows much,' said Paul.

'I think somebody should tell him it isn't polite to sit on the table,' said Kate.

However, there wasn't time to think about the conservationist any further. They had to clean up and make their beds, and Kate had to iron her skirt and blouse.

Then Jock arrived.

'Come on,' he said. 'We'll be late.'

The kids quickly got their bikes. The morning was sparkling, clear and fresh. As soon as they reached the main road, they could see that almost everyone on Falcon Island was out today. There were more people and cars on the road than they had ever seen before, except for the time when Herbie Brown had got drunk and had climbed up on to the hotel roof and wouldn't come down.

Cars whizzed past – Mr Meredith, Mrs Pike, the Adamsons, the Morellis – from every part of the island people were streaming towards the hall where the meeting would take place.

'I wonder what old Brady will think of all this,' said Paul.

'I reckon he's chickened out,' said Jock.

'How's that?' said Paul.

'He's got the sulks, I bet,' said Kate with a giggle.

'Don't know about that,' said Jock. 'But Grandpop and I saw him going to his boat this morning when we went to open up the hall and put out the chairs. And he was in his best suit,' Jock added.

'What!' exclaimed Paul. 'Why was he in his suit?'

'Don't know,' said Jock. 'But he's still out in his boat.'

Paul had a feeling that there was something not quite right about all of this. Why wasn't Brady going to the hall to put his point of view? It was very unlike Brady.

'What about the guy he met last night? Did you see him?'

'No. There was no one with him,' said Jock.

'I think there's something wrong,' said Paul. 'I'm going to get Dad's binoculars and see what he's doing out there.'

'But we'll be late,' said Kate.

'Don't care,' said Paul. 'I want to see what Brady's doing.'

While the other two waited, Paul rode back to the house and got his father's binoculars from the cupboard in his bedroom.

When he returned they all rode quickly to the hill that overlooked the bay. They could see Brady's boat some distance away, out on the water. Paul trained the binoculars on to Brady's boat. He could see it quite clearly. It was chugging along very slowly.

'Well, he's coming towards the island,' said Paul. Then he saw a second figure on Brady's boat. He could make out a dark-haired man sitting in the stern. He wore a bright red shirt.

'Are you sure Brady was by himself this morning?' said Paul.

'I told you – there was no one with him. Why?' asked Jock.

'Well – there's somebody with him now.'

'Old Brady is having a lot of visitors this weekend,' said Kate.

'I'm beginning to wonder why,' said Paul.

'I know!' said Jock. 'I'll bet you anything he's bringing somebody from the sand mining company.'

'I think you're right,' said Paul. Then he added thoughtfully, 'I think we'd better tell Dad. Come on!'

At the hall, while the kids were watching Brady, a crowd outside had gathered around Mike Jarvis, who was now playing to the hilt his role of visiting celebrity and authority. He had made a very pronounced impression on everyone. Mrs Yates was in a bit of a dither.

'It's so nice to meet you, Mr Carter,' she said. 'We're all delighted to have such a distinguished guest. In fact we are very flattered. It did occur to me that you might be able to stay afterwards and I could show you items of historical interest – we do have quite a significant monument in the town square and. . . .'

'Dorothy!' said Frank. She'd been monopolising the conservationist for the past ten minutes. But Mrs Yates didn't take any notice.

'Of course one of my major concerns is to make sure that this sand-mining idea doesn't interfere in any way with our historical heritage – a point you might like to add to the rest of the things you intend to talk about, Mr Carter.'

'Yes. Yes,' said Mike Jarvis.

'Dorothy!' said Frank firmly, when it looked as if Mrs Yates was to go on further. 'We'd better get this meeting started.'

Mrs Yates looked peeved at Frank. She had taken rather a fancy to Mike Jarvis.

Frank ushered Mike Jarvis into the hall and led him to the dais, where there was a table and two chairs.

Everybody was filing inside and sitting down. In five minutes Falcon Island Hall was bulging at the seams. Frank, standing on the dais, looked about with satisfaction. It was the best turnout for years. Frank nodded to Miss Fitzgerald who was sitting at the front. As Secretary of the Community Association, she was going to take notes. Vicki smiled at him. The response to their call for the Community to get together had been very pleasing.

Frank could see that the people had more or less divided into two groups. Those who would oppose the sand mining at any cost were sitting on one side, and those who had forcefully spoken up in favour of Jack Brady's move in the pub during the week were in a bunch on the other.

The gathering was a good thing, thought Frank. Everyone would have the opportunity to hear what the problems were likely to be and then they could weigh the matter up and decide whether increased economic prosperity was worth the price for some environmental change. Whatever the result, only discussion and examination of the problems could lead to a democratic outcome. Frank scanned the faces again. Then he became aware of a person missing. Jack Brady. Frank was disappointed. Old Jack should have been here. People would want to hear his side. That would only be fair. Beside him there was a slight cough, and Mike Jarvis said:

'You'd better introduce me, I suppose – get underway.' He didn't want to delay much longer. He was starting to feel a little nervous.

'Yes,' said Frank. He stood up and rapped the table.

The hall fell silent. Then Frank began.

'It's good so see so many friends and neighbours here,' he said.

There was a general buzz of good-natured agreement and applause.

'As you know,' said Frank, 'the Falcon Island Community Association has called this meeting to discuss the problems that might face us if a proposal to mine beach sands in Geelup Cove goes ahead.'

'The best thing that could happen!'

'Shame!'

'Never!' Various voices rang out.

Frank spoke up a little more loudly. 'Today the Committee of the Falcon Island Community Association hope to get your opinions to guide us in the decisions we will have to make – whether as a community we will oppose sand mining, or whether we will find in favour of it. To give us expert advice, I would now like to introduce Mr John Carter, a distinguished conservationist, who has kindly agreed to speak to us.'

Frank sat down. There was a generous round of applause. Mike Jarvis took a drink of water from the glass on the table. Then he got to his feet. He acknowledged the clapping with a smiling bow.

'I think this guy is a bit of a performer,' said Alf in an undertone.

'Ssh,' said Nan.

'Well, Ladies and Gentlemen,' Mike Jarvis began, 'I always believe that one must make a careful judgement before a decision is made.

'Hear, hear!' said Herb.

'I second that,' said Mrs Yates.

The town square was deserted as the children pedalled furiously past the monument.

'We're going to be really late,' panted Paul.

'We'll make it,' said Jock.

Out in the bay, Brady was enjoying the morning sunshine. In fact he thought it was a pity that he hadn't brought his fishing gear. It was good fishing weather. His boat chugged along, almost dead slow. He glanced at the young man sitting on a fish box, blinking behind his steel-rimmed glasses and looking at his watch. Brady smiled to himself. He hadn't had so much fun for years.

John Carter looked at his watch again, as he had been doing almost every thirty seconds in the last quarter of an hour. He was beginning to wonder if they would ever get to the island. This boat seemed to have the facility of running its engine but not going forward. Finally he said,

'It was very good of you to pick me up, Mr Brady, but. . . .'

'Call me Jack,' Brady broke in, cheerfully.

'It's very good of you, Jack, to bring me over. . . .'

'The Committee thought that it would be more friendly if you were picked up by somebody,' said Brady. He almost chuckled out loud. He wondered how his mate Mike Jarvis was getting on.

'But it's five past eleven already,' said John Carter anxiously. 'Can you get your boat to go a little faster?'

'Don't you worry,' said Brady soothingly. 'Meetings on the island never get started on time.'

'But we're late. . . .'

'Wouldn't want to push this old boat,' said Brady jovially, 'Might come apart at the seams.'

'Oh no!' exclaimed John Carter in despair.

The kids had reached the hall. They threw down their bikes and rushed up the steps. But they were too late. They could see as they squeezed into the back seat that there wouldn't be any chance to tell Frank that Brady was possibly bringing over Mr Scott from the sand mining company.

It took a moment or two to get their bearings. Then they realised that the whole of the hall was filled with people looking at one another, puzzled and concerned. The object of their bewilderment was obviously the conservationist who was standing on the dais. And they could see that Frank was perturbed, but was keeping an outer air of calm. But as soon as they heard what the conservationist was saying, they understood.

Mike Jarvis was now warming to his task – the presentation of the advantages of ilmenite, as Brady had said.

'You see,' said Mike Jarvis, facing the audience in the hall, 'beach sand – this special beach sand is a commodity in worldwide demand. The beaches of Falcon Island have a great resource. . . .'

'We know that,' shouted Alf. 'Get to the point – will it harm our environment or not?'

'Yeah – get to the point,' said another voice.

'Shut up and let him speak!' said Joe, a small man who was sitting down the front.

'Quiet!' roared Mr Meredith.

'Order! Order!' said Frank, who had been trying to maintain some sort of calm for the past five minutes, and was now becoming quite worried. This conservationist didn't seem to know much.

'What's going on?' whispered Paul to Jock.

'Don't know,' said Jock.

But it was very apparent that something was wrong.

'If the ilmenite on Falcon Island proves to be a large deposit,' said Mike Jarvis, 'we have a problem of responsibility. Now, I ask, which is the greater evil, denying the world this commodity or saving part of a very small island? Small in world terms, I mean.'

'Whose side is he on?' whispered Paul.

But Jock's reply was drowned by Mrs Yates standing on her feet and declaring, 'Falcon Island is the most important place in the world for those of us who live here! And I for one won't see it sullied by industry.' Mrs Yates had forgotten her earlier admiration for the conservationist – she was now flushed and annoyed.

'Of course . . . there are always two points of view,' said Mike Jarvis soothingly. At that point he coughed. It was a harsh, dry cough as if he had an irritating tickle in his chest. Then he coughed again. He had to take a sip of water.

Paul had heard the cough. Suddenly it clicked. He jumped to his feet. Kate and Jock were taken by surprise.

'Quick – Quick! Come with me,' said Paul as he stumbled over people and shot out of the hall. Jock and Kate, not quite knowing what was going on, followed him, half falling over people's feet.

Outside Paul was already on his bike when the other two joined him.

'What's going on?' demanded Jock.

'That guy in there,' said Paul. 'He's no conservationist! He's Brady's mate from last night!'

'What!' said Jock.

'And the real conservationist is out on Brady's boat, I bet.'

'What are we waiting for?' said Jock. 'Quick – the *Urchin*!'

Out in the bay, Brady's boat had given a last asthmatic cough and splutter some minutes before. The engine had failed and died.

'What's happened now?' cried an agitated John Carter.

'She'll be all right,' said Brady cheerfully. 'Temperamental, this boat – never know what she's gonna do.' Particularly if the fuel line has been switched off, he could have added.

'Can you fix it?' said John Carter, anxiously mopping his brow.

'Yeah – yeah. Get her going in a tick,' said Brady. He gave a little chuckle. This was better than the telly, he thought.

The kids had reached the jetty and were pounding along its rough, uneven planks.

'Brady seems to have stopped. His boat isn't moving!' called Jock.

'Let's see why,' said Paul.

They piled into the *Urchin*. Jock started the outboard motor.

In Brady's boat, Brady was ineffectually tinkering with the fuel line. He pulled a grave face.

'Fuel line,' he said solemnly.

'That's bad, isn't it?' said John Carter.

'Could be,' said Brady. Then, as if thinking hard, he said, 'Must be in the back of the tank.'

'Can't you blow in the pipe or something?'

'Waste of time,' said Brady. 'Wouldn't do any good at all.' He shook his head as if solving this problem was going to take some time.

Carter slumped down, defeated. Brady, with a sly smile, began fiddling with the petrol bowl and then, taking a spanner, started to unscrew various nuts and bolts. At this rate, Brady thought, he could do this all day long. He wondered again how Mike was getting along. He could just imagine it – Mike in the hall. It would certainly give those islanders something to think about. He almost laughed out loud.

John Carter sat on the smelly fish box in blank resignation. He felt completely frustrated. He had spent two evenings preparing his address. The conservation of sand dunes was his special subject, and now it appeared that he had probably lost the chance to interest the people who might have cared.

But suddenly he both saw and heard a small boat in the bay, skimming across the water. He jumped to his feet.

'Help! Help!' he shouted.

This move took Brady entirely by surprise. He lifted his head to see what was happening. In doing so he banged it violently on the top of the raised engine cowling.

'Criiiiipes!' he said, rubbing his head, his eyes watering.

Then he saw who it was that Carter was trying to signal.

'Those kids!' And they were coming straight for them. Brady fumbled desperately, trying to reassemble parts of his engine.

'Wave! Wave!' Carter shouted at Brady.

'They can hear you,' said Brady sourly.

And the kids could. Jock brought the *Urchin* around so that it came alongside Brady's boat.

'Hi there, Mr Brady!' called Paul.

'My gosh, I'm glad to see you!' said John Carter.

'Broken down have you, Mr Brady?' asked Jock.

Kate giggled as Brady glared.

'What does it look like?' growled Brady.

'It doesn't look too good to me,' said Jock, managing to keep his face serious. Kate giggled again. Old Brady looked so furious!

'Lucky we saw you,' said Paul. 'We can tow you in.'

'No you will not!' exploded Brady. 'Clear off and mind your own business! Go on, clear off!'

'Hey – just a minute!' said John Carter in alarm. 'I'd like to prevail on these kids to give me a lift. I've got a meeting to get to.'

The kids exchanged knowing glances. 'It's in the hall,' he said. 'And I'm already at least twenty minutes late. . . .'

'Of course we'll give you a lift,' said Paul. 'Hop in.'

John Carter gratefully clambered into the *Urchin*, as Brady looked on with a sickly smile. He knew when he was beaten.

'See you, Mr Brady!' said the kids as Jock revved up the motor.

'Would you like us to come back and get you. Mr Brady?' said Paul.

'No thanks!' said Brady. He looked as if he'd like to wring their necks.

The *Urchin* pulled away from Brady's boat. John Carter settled himself.

'A funny fellow, that Mr Brady,' he said.

The kids looked solemn.

'He means well,' said Paul.

Kate started to laugh. She was remembering Brady's face.

Chapter 9

On their way to the hall, Mr Carter explained to the kids what had happened. He had been waiting on the mainland jetty for the ferry when Jack Brady came up and introduced himself as a representative of the island community. Within no time Mr Carter found himself on Brady's boat and they were heading for Falcon Island. And then, of course, his troubles began.

Everyone turned to look as the kids ushered Mr Carter into the hall. Up on the dais Mike Jarvis was still talking plausibly around in circles.

'Dad!' Paul called out, interrupting. 'This is the real Mr Carter! That bloke up there is one of Brady's mates!'

'What!' said Frank.

A collective gasp went through the hall, as John Carter said, 'I'm Mr Carter. . . .'

Jarvis, seeing it was all up, tried to make a bolt for the door. Alf, pretty spry for an old chap, grabbed him. Then a wild uproar broke out. Mr Meredith ineffectually tried to collar Jarvis, but was prevented by Harry.

Mrs Pike was twittering and fluttering around. 'My goodness! My goodness!' was all she could say, but Mrs Yates was so enraged that she snatched up Mrs Mortimer's sunshade and advanced upon a cowering and terrified Mike Jarvis as if she were about to impale him.

'I'll teach you to make fools of us!' she said, stabbing in Mike Jarvis's direction. She was also in danger of stabbing Alf.

'Hold on, Dorothy!' said Frank. 'Mind out for Alf!'

It took a bit of trouble to calm Mrs Yates.

In the meantime, Mrs Mortimer had started to dab her eyes.

'I thought the conservationist was a very nice person,' she said. 'I can't believe he isn't true.'

In the middle of it all stood John Carter, blinking and bewildered.

The people in the hall now split into two distinct groups – those for sand mining and those against. And they all started arguing with one another. There were fights breaking out like sparks from a bushfire, and the conflagration was growing. To add to the confusion, Brady turned up to collect Jarvis.

He was quite unperturbed.

'Golly, this is better than the TV!' said Jock to Paul, in an undertone.

'Come on, mate!' said Brady to Mike Jarvis.

'What a nerve you've got!' said Mrs Yates, still in a state.

'Aw, shut up!' Brady said. 'The trouble with you econuts – you can't see a good thing when it's staring you in the face. You deserve the place to fold up altogether.'

'You should be run out of town,' said Mrs Yates.

'It's still a free country,' said Brady as he hauled Jarvis through the door.

After things began to quieten down a bit, Frank invited the proper Mr Carter to give his address. Unfortunately, by now Mr Carter's talk was something of an anticlimax, although the points he made were considered and pertinent. Sand mining did destroy beach fronts; however, sand mining companies were obliged to operate as carefully as they could and they had to restore the site. This was all strictly controlled by law. Nevertheless, the birds and animals of the area would be disturbed, and the same applied to the ecology, and of course the appearance of the beach front would be changed forever – something the islanders must bear in mind if they wanted to continue to attract tourists to the island.

When Mr Carter had finished, Mr Meredith got to his feet.

'It seems to me that out Committee should be asked to maintain close contact with the sand mining company in order to watch over our interests.'

'Hear! Hear!' said a large number of the people in the hall.

After that, Mr Carter was thanked for his time and trouble, some people left to go home, but a group lingered on talking about it all. Feelings were still running high.

Paul, Jock and Kate got their bikes to ride home. Somehow, to the kids, it all seemed so inconclusive. They had expected that Brady would have been told that he couldn't go ahead with his sand mine, and that would be the end of it. But it hadn't worked out like that.

'I think quite a few people want the sand mine,' said Kate.

'And they like old Brady's cheek,' said Paul. He was remembering fragments of conversation and argument he had heard in the hall.

'Well – what's going to happen?'

'I don't think anybody knows yet,' said Paul.

Later that day Frank rang Bob Scott of the Barron-West Sand Mining Company. As Paul and Kate were in the kitchen they could easily hear what was being said. Frank told Mr Scott what Brady had done, and by the way the conversation went, it seemed that Mr Scott was very perturbed by Brady's underhand behaviour. Frank and Mr Scott talked about the problems of mining Geelup Cove at some length. Frank sketched in the things that worried people most – basically, heavy trucks passing through the settlement, sand blowing down into the township, and the loss of the safest beach close to the town.

When Frank hung up he said to Kate and Paul,

'Mr Scott is coming over tomorrow. We'll have a

special Committee meeting tomorrow morning. He said he might be able to offer some alternative suggestions.'

'Like what?' said Paul. 'Building a jetty in Geelup Cove instead of using the town jetty, I bet. That would mean blasting the reef and spoiling the bay.'

Frank looked worried.

'That might be a proposal,' he said. He sighed. 'Whatever happens, it will be impossible to please everyone.'

'I wish old Brady knew how much he's upset the whole island,' said Kate.

'If it hadn't been Jack Brady it would have been someone else eventually,' said Frank. 'The problem is there's ilmenite on the island and that means there will inevitably be mainland interest once that fact is known. How we manage it for the best is what I'm concerned about.'

The next morning was Sunday, the day the kids were to go diving with Vim in Dutchman's Bay. It was about nine o'clock when they met him at the jetty.

'How was the meeting yesterday?' asked Vim as Jock handed him his air tank and their towels and swimsuits.

They told him what had happened. Jock filled out the story more than a bit to make it sound as if Mike Jarvis had come close to being impaled and disembowelled by Mrs Yates wielding Mrs Mortimer's sunshade.

'Too bad I missed the fun!' said Vim.

'You should have been there,' said Kate firmly. 'We needed all our friends.'

'You seemed to manage all right,' he laughed. 'The way you outwitted Brady!'

Unexpectedly Paul felt an irrational rush of sadness. Didn't Vim care what might happen to the island? Why didn't he want to be involved?

'Ready now?' said Vim. 'Paul, unhitch the mooring line and we're away.'

As they came out of the bay, and left the leeward side of the island, the water was a sparkling blue-green. The sky was clear with no clouds – there was no hint yet that summer would soon be passing, and the serene nature of the sea would change to the grey storms of winter.

The tone of the *Isabella*'s engines took on a deeper note as she thrust her way powerfully through the low swell. They were passing other boats, holiday people out for a day's fishing. Before long they had left most of them behind, and they were now in sight of Dirk's rock which was fairly close to Dutchman's Bay.

Paul was beside Vim in the wheelhouse. They hadn't spoken for a while, then Vim said quietly, 'I had a good reason for not coming to the meeting yesterday.'

'Oh,' said Paul, flushing, feeling uncomfortable. Vim had obviously sensed how he had felt.

'Yes,' said Vim, ignoring Paul's self-consciousness, 'I've been diving every day this week in Dutchman's Bay.'

'Every day? Why? Have you found something?'

'No. But I think that I will. I've got an old chart that makes me think Dutchman's Bay is where the *Golden Falcon* went down.'

'But you had charts before. . . .'

'Yes – I know, and I've been looking for the old wreck all around the island for months, but now – I think I'm on the right track at last. I've had some old records copied and sent out from Holland and I've been translating them.'

'Why do you have to translate them?' said Paul. 'Aren't they in Dutch?'

'They are in old Dutch, which is just about as difficult to decipher as a foreign language, even if you know modern Dutch,' Vim said. His voice was excited. 'I've found out a lot more about the storm and what happened when the *Golden Falcon* was lost. The *Isabella* followed her for some time until they heard the boom of cannon. It was the *Golden Falcon* giving them a warning – because of the reefs. It's really fantastic to read.'

'But do they say the *Golden Falcon* went down in Dutchman's Bay?' asked Paul.

'No,' said Vim. 'But I've got a chart that has given me some bearings to work on, and I've worked out the distances recorded in the old sea logs. Everything seems to point to Dutchman's Bay. I'm determined I'm not going to let those old Dutch guys defeat us. We're going to find that wreck!' He looked at Paul with a grin. 'We will, won't we?'

Paul felt a whole weight of unhappiness lift. He felt reassured. Vim cared for the island in his own way. But he had to express it in the way that held most meaning for him, which was to search for the wreck and to find the secret that the island reefs had held for so long.

At about ten thirty, Frank went down to the jetty to meet Mr Scott. As they shook hands, Mr Scott said, 'I'm sorry for the way Mr Brady has handled the matter. It has always been our company's policy to meet local people half way.'

'Brady's in it to make a few dollars,' said Frank.

'Well – of course we are too,' said Mr Scott. 'But we like to think that we act responsibly. Anyway, I'm here to see if we can come up with a solution to some of the problems.'

'Access to Geelup Cove is our main concern – we don't want trucks going through the town.'

'Well – we'll see what we can sort out.'

Then they drove to the school where the Committee – Miss Fitzgerald, Mrs Yates, Harry Maxwell the publican and Alf – were waiting for them.

As they sat down, Frank said, 'I went around to see Jack Brady this morning and asked him to come and talk things over, but he told me to shove off – only not so politely.'

They all laughed except Mr Scott, who looked bothered.

'That sounds like Jack!' said Harry.

'Mr Brady should be here,' said Mr Scott. 'He doesn't show the right attitude.'

Frank and Alf both felt some sympathy for Mr Scott. He was used to proper procedures, but on the island people didn't worry about things like that. They went by rule of thumb.

While they listened, Mr Scott outlined his company's policies. He stressed that they adhered very strictly to the regulations about rehabilitation of the sand dunes. Then he repeated what he had said to Frank – that they had no wish to cause dissension in the community.

'In that case,' said Mrs Yates, rather overwhelming the Grade Four chair she was sitting on, 'Go and mine somewhere else.'

Mr Scott looked a little pained.

'I understand your feelings, Mrs Yates,' he said. 'But I'm afraid that that isn't possible. We still have a feasibility study to do, but we are fairly confident that we will prove the site to have a commercial potential.'

'As I thought! A violator!' hissed Mrs Yates in an undertone to Miss Fitzgerald.

'Dorothy – no emotion,' said Frank. 'Let's get all the facts.'

Mrs Yates looked blackly rebellious. 'Some people have feelings. . . .' she began, but Alf intervened.

'What if we put up opposition to your sand mining proposals?' he asked.

'We hope that you won't,' said Mr Scott.

'But what if we did?' persisted Alf. Alf was summing up this Mr Scott. Although he was polite and prepared to cooperate with them, Alf could see that he was quite a determined person under his pleasant manner.

'You would have to have a very good argument against us,' said Mr Scott. 'A very good argument,' he stressed.

'Do you mean', said Alf slowly, 'that we have very

little chance of stopping your company from mining on the island?'

There was a pause. Then Mr Scott's answer was to the point.

'To be perfectly frank, Mr Dixon – you have no chance at all.'

There was a stunned silence. Even Mrs Yates was lost for words. It had been the quiet hope of both Frank and Alf that if they managed to get enough support from the islanders they could prevent mining from taking place.

'We are acting completely within the law,' said Mr Scott.

'But we don't want sand mining,' said Mrs Yates.

Mr Scott appeared to consider for a moment.

'Of course there is the other deposit on Falcon Island,' he said slowly. 'Although we think it has more problems. . . .'

'What other deposit?' demanded Frank and Alf.

'Didn't you know?' said Mr Scott, surprised. 'I discussed the matter at length with Mr Brady . . . didn't he . . . Oh!' He saw the faces around him.

There was uproar again.

'He kept that quiet!' said Frank.

'He's a tricky beggar,' said Alf bitterly.

'He's a moral leper, you mean!' said Mrs Yates in indignation.

'He knows what he's doing,' said Harry.

'But where is it?' said Alf.

'Dutchman's Bay,' said Mr Scott.

'Dutchman's Bay!' said Frank. 'Council land!'

The Committee was silenced again. This was certainly a very different proposition. And Frank realised that the royalties for the lease could go direct to the community itself – a real boost to the income of the island.

'It has big problems,' said Mr Scott. 'But then, so of course does Geelup Cove. Of course, we have known about both deposits for some time – it just hasn't been economically worthwhile to worry about them until now. But the price in the world market has risen – now it's a good prospect.'

Frank and Alf fell into a short private discussion. But Mrs Yates had become very agitated.

'You can't mine in Dutchman's Bay,' she said. 'It's the site of our famous wreck.'

'What wreck?' asked Mr Scott.

'Nobody knows where the mystery wreck is,' said Harry, 'or if it exists.'

'Of course it exists,' said Mrs Yates. 'It's the fabric of our historical heritage.'

'It's a legend – a myth,' said Harry.

'I beg to disagree,' began Mrs Yates.

'Look – don't let's start a fight about whether the *Golden Falcon* exists or not,' said Frank, who had finished hastily conferring with Alf. 'Our problem is to make sure that the town site and settlement are not disturbed, and as an added bonus. . . .' But he wasn't allowed to finish.

'You're not going to allow yourself to be compromised, are you, Frank?' demanded Mrs Yates. 'Of course the *Golden Falcon* exists.'

'Compromised?' said Frank. 'What do you mean?'

'Knuckling under to big business – that's what I mean,' said Mrs Yates.

'I've got a responsibility to the whole island,' said Frank heatedly. It looked as if things were set for a fight.

Mr Scott interrupted. In a diplomatic tone he put forward a suggestion. 'Why don't we look at both sites? Then your community can give us a proposal about which location is most suitable from your point of view. As I said – we are ready to cooperate with you if we can.'

'I agree to that!' said Harry.

'Why don't we go and check the sites now?' said Alf.

'It'll take a lot to convince me that sand mining should take place in Dutchman's Bay,' said Mrs Yates.

They all sighed. 'Come on, Dorothy. . . .' said Alf.

On the western side of the island in the bay now under such contentious discussion, the *Isabella* was riding serenely at anchor.

Paul and Kate had only been to Dutchman's Bay once before, Jock never. It was very different from gentle Geelup Cove. It was a semicircular shape. To the north there were tall granite cliffs with pillars of black stone which tumbled into the sea in huge slabs like the ruins of an ancient fortress; to the south there were enormous jagged rocks that seemed to stand like sentinels at the fortress wall. These two arms curved to enclose a small natural harbour, guarded from behind by a series of undulating sand dunes that seemed like giant steps. The ridge of the sand dunes was covered with a thick, dense heath unbroken against the sky. Altogether the entire scale of Dutchman's Bay was broader and much grander than Geelup Cove where they usually went to dive.

'Gosh! This is a super place,' said Jock.

'Haven't you been here before?' said Vim.

'No, but it's fantastic!' said Jock.

The beach looked a wonderful place to explore, but Vim was impatient to begin diving. The conditions grew rough in the afternoon, even though the bay was sheltered.

'You can look around later,' he said. 'But we must get down to the real business, searching the caverns. . . .'

Vim explained what he wanted done.

'To do the job properly', he said, 'we will have to chart and check the entire sea bed. A big job, and we've only got a few weeks to do it in before the first autumn storms. Then we won't be able to dive – the sea stirs up the sand, it's difficult to see, and it gets dangerous. So we haven't got much time.'

Vim explained how they would have to take a note of where anything was found. He then found several wax pencils and thick plastic sheets.

'These are your underwater notepads,' he said, giving one to each of the boys. 'When you find something you write the details on this plastic sheet. Then later I'll mark our finds on a chart so that we have a complete record of what we do.'

Jock and Paul were both very excited. Now they were about to dive and to do a proper underwater search. Paul was so elated that he felt a little sick with excitement. Who knew what they would find? And if they found the wreck, what would they find then? He'd never let his imagination get that far before. Silver coins, perhaps some gold? Or some precious ornaments? They could all be down there under the sea.

'You'll need a dive bag each,' said Vim, as he took several from a locker. They were made of strong yellow nylon mesh.

As Kate watched the preparation, she felt a bit upset and left out. The boys were so lucky, she thought. She was determined that when she was older she too would dive, so that she could be part of it all.

Once they were zipped up in their wet suits, Vim made the boys go through all their safety signals again. After a double check of the equipment they at last moved to the stern of the *Isabella*. One after the other they went into the sea. The big adventure was about to begin!

Vim was in the lead. He indicated that they should enter the deep grotto just ahead. They swam through a tunnel, disturbing a shoal of herring and several rainbow-coloured parrot fish. Ahead there was an indented reef face. Vim swam about three metres. Then he indicated that Paul and Jock were to start a systematic exploration of the reef from the tunnel to that point.

Where do we begin? Paul thought. The area seemed vast. The filtered sunlight, catching some patches of weed and rock, leaving other areas in darkness, seemed to add an even further dimension of mystery. Begin! Paul told himself. This might be it!

In Geelup Cove, Mrs Yates was beginning to regret that she had decided to come with the rest of them to assess the potential of the sand mining site. Already her shoes were full of sand, her nose was sunburnt, she was out of breath, and she had torn her slacks in getting over Jack Brady's barbed wire fence. The combination of these trials, with the indignity of puffing way behind the others, was making her wish that Jack Brady could have something unpleasant befall him very soon. Mr Scott, however, seemed to be indefatigable, as he nimbly led them over sandhill after sandhill, discussing all the problems without so much as a bead of perspiration on his brow.

Still, a citizen must be a citizen, thought Mrs Yates as Harry, Frank or Miss Fitzgerald came to haul her upwards yet again. Mr Scott had now launched into the problems of building a jetty in Geelup Cove. He stood at the top of the limestone cliffs, looking down. To Mrs Yates the sea looked unbearably enticing. If only she could go down for a quick little dip and a paddle . . . but she had to listen to Mr Scott saying:

'The major problem here would be in blasting the reef so that large boats could come in. Then we would have to dredge the Cove as well – very expensive indeed. It would be much cheaper for us to upgrade the island jetty and use that and then build a new road around the settlement, rather than come through the town. That way we would avoid the school and the town centre altogether.'

'You've considered that, have you?' asked Frank.

'We are considering everything at the moment,' said Mr Scott.

With that he led them to the furthest point of Brady's land so that they could see how the sand dunes would be affected on the town side and what problems there might be in sand blowing down into the settlement.

'I can't see that blowing sand is a real problem,' said Mr Scott. 'It would be against the prevailing wind.'

Wearily, Mrs Yates pushed damp tendrils of hair under her scarf.

'Are you all right, Dorothy?' said Frank.

'Are you sure you can manage?' said Vicki Fitzgerald.

'Yes, dear,' said Mrs Yates grimly. 'Our duty must be done.'

'This is all a bit much for you, Mrs Yates,' said Mr Scott.

'No. Not at all,' lied Mrs Yates.

With that they all plunged downwards again, into thick scrub. Branches snatched and clutched at Mrs Yates – how she longed to be in her nice sunroom with a cool drink, ready to watch a good film on TV – the usual thing she did on Sunday. But still, she mustn't weaken.

Suddenly Miss Fitzgerald, who was a bit ahead, called to Frank.

'What's that?'

They listened. There was the sound of an axe striking wood, which changed to the high-piched buzz of a chain saw.

'Somebody's chopping wood!'

'That's in the Reserve!' said Alf. 'What's going on?'

Mrs Yates honestly didn't care. But she followed the others, who headed off in the direction of the sound of the chain saw.

Mrs Yates was the last to see what was happening as they all burst through the scrub. But Frank had taken it in. He was livid with rage. It looked as if a small tornado had been through the bush – trees were down, limbs and branches strewn in all directions.

The culprit with the chain saw in his hand was quite unmoved by Frank's fury.

'What the hell are you doing?' demanded Frank.

'What does it look like?' said Brady.

'It looks like public vandalism,' said Miss Fitzgerald.

'And it looks as if you're trying to widen the track that leads into your property to give better access to the sand,' said Alf, as angry as Frank.

'You're dead right,' said Jack Brady.

Mrs Yates now saw what had appalled the others.

'You can't do that, Jack Brady!' she said.

'I've just done it!' said Brady.

'You've gone too far this time, Jack!' said Alf, enraged.

Mr Scott took over.

'Mr Brady, you seem to forget that our arrangements haven't been finalised yet. Starting a road is premature.'

'We've got a contract – you signed it,' said Brady.

'I took out an option with you for three months,' said Mr Scott. 'That means we have yet to make final arrangements.'

It was Brady's turn to get mad.

'You've been got at by this bunch of thick-headed nitwits,' he said.

'Just a minute,' said Mr Scott, his voice a little high. His training in public relations and management had left him unprepared for problems like this.

'Get . . . lost, the lot of you!' said Brady with a rude gesture.

Mr Scott looked bewildered.

'Just a minute, Mr Brady,' he said. But he was talking to Brady's retreating back.

'How uncouth!' said Mrs Yates.

Brady got into his truck. He turned the engine on and slammed it into reverse. But this time he had mis-calculated. His wheels started to churn. Great clouds of blinding dust flew up. The wheels spun but he didn't move. Dust practically obscured Brady's truck and the noise was deafening.

'He's bogged down. Serves him right,' said Mrs Yates.

Frank started to run up the road. He reached the truck.

'We'll give you a push, he said.

'No,' said Brady.

'Don't be like that,' said Frank. 'We'll give you a hand.'

'No,' said Brady.

'Don't do anything for him, Frank!' cried Mrs Yates.

'Come on, Jack, get out and we'll push you.'

Glaring, Brady got out.

'Now, Dorothy,' said Frank. 'You get in and steer, and we'll push.'

'Me?' said Mrs Yates.

'Yes. Come on.'

Mrs Yates saw her chance. She'd let Brady know what was what.

'This is what community cooperation is all about,' she said to Brady, with a suddenly acquired sweet tone. 'You can achieve anything with a bit of cooperation.'

'Never mind that, Dorothy,' said Frank. 'Just get in.'

Mrs Yates condescended to get into the driver's seat. She clambered in with as much dignity and flourish as she could muster. Then she had to adjust her scarf, her sunglasses, the driving seat, and the seat belt.

'Don't worry about the seat belt, Dorothy,' said Harry with a wink. 'You're not going far.'

'I have to do it all the right way,' said Mrs Yates with yet another knowing look at Brady. Brady was suddenly feeling this wasn't his best day.

'Ready now,' called Mrs Yates at last.

'Turn her on then,' said Frank.

Mrs Yates hunted along the dashboard and found the key..

'It's been years . . .' she said. But she didn't manage to finish. Frank and Alf and Mr Scott and Miss Fitzgerald and Harry, and a somewhat reluctant Brady, went to the back.

'Right – now!' said Frank. 'Accelerate!'

As Mrs Yates shoved her foot hard on to the accelerator, the team at the back strained and heaved. The engine roared, but the truck didn't budge.

'Stop, everybody!' Frank said. They stopped pushing.

'Dorothy!' said Frank.

'Yes, Frank,' said Mrs Yates.

'Put it in gear, Dorothy . . . please.'

'Oh! Of course. . . .' clucked Mrs Yates.

'And – is the handbrake off?'

There was a little pause.

'It is now, Frank,' said Mrs Yates.

'Well – let's try again,' said Frank to the rest of them.

'O.K. . . . altogether . . . now!'

The truck miraculously sprang into life, and in the process a veritable sandstorm showered them from head to foot with fine black sand. None of them could see. They coughed and spluttered, eyes streaming. But as they wiped their eyes, they heard an enraged bellow.

'Stop! Stop! Me truck! You stupid woman! It was Brady in anguish running down the road, as Mrs Yates, sunglasses slipping, drove Brady's truck – a truck that seemed to be possessed with all the joy of a spring lamb as it leapt and skipped and bounded down the track.

'Stop! Stop!' roared Brady, hitching up his pants as he ran. But all was in vain. Mrs Yates was losing command. The truck bucked and jerked and bounced from one side of the track to the other.

'Stop! Please – me truck,' pleaded Brady in despair.

What might have happened nobody knows, for at that moment Mrs Yates saw her chance. Ahead was a large patch of loose sand. With unerring aim she made for it. The truck's wheels dragged. The engine began to cough. It spluttered, hiccoughed, and eventually died.

As the rest of them arrived, panting, Mrs Yates climbed out of the truck.

'It's bogged down,' she announced unnecessarily.

Brady was practically wringing his hands.

'The blasted woman has bogged it again!' he said.

'There's no need to take umbrage, Mr Brady,' said Mrs Yates. 'Thanks would be more in order.'

'Wow!' said Brady weakly. It was all he could manage.

Chapter 10

In Dutchman's Bay Vim, Paul and Jock had been exploring the grotto all morning. They had carefully checked a great deal of the cavern, the reef walls and the seabed, which was marked Exploration Area One on Vim's chart. They worked as a team, Paul and Jock bearing in mind the things that Vim had told them to watch for, such as discoloured patches on the coral, which could indicate the presence of metal, and the presence of any sea growth in horizontal lines. Vim had explained that nature rarely makes a straight line, and therefore any geometrical shape beneath the surface of the sea could indicate cannon, spars, anchors or the keel of a boat.

From time to time they surfaced to hand what they had found to Kate, who labelled each item as it was given to her. But their finds weren't very significant – only an old corroded fish knife, a variety of rusty fish hooks, and some broken cray pots.

After an hour or so, Vim gave the signal to surface.

'Not much in there,' said Jock, emptying his dive bag when they were back on deck. He had brought up some sponges and coral.

'Don't be disappointed,' Vim said. 'Exploring is like that – you can search for weeks, even months, then suddenly, when you least expect it, you find something. That's why it's so exciting.'

'If only we had a bit more to go on,' said Paul. 'Do the old records give you latitude and longitude?'

Vim shook his head. 'It's difficult,' he said. 'Translating is very slow work. Most of the letters and diaries give details about the food and conditions, occasionally they mention how far they travelled that day, from time to time there's a mention of a bearing from the stars. The log book from the old *Isabella* helps a lot – what I'm doing is working out their positions and transferring that to a modern map. The more I translate, the more the details fit together, and everything points to Dutchman's Bay.'

'Well,' said Jock, 'it's going to take a long time doing this exploring. We'd better get on with it.'

'Lunch first,' said Vim.

'Hurray!' said Kate. 'Let's have a picnic on the beach.'

'What if I show you how to cook fish Hawaiian style?' said Vim.

'Great!' said Paul.

In a few minutes they had packed a cardboard box with everything they would need and were rowing ashore in Vim's rubber dinghy.

The beach was untouched, washed level and smooth. The only marks on it were the footprints of seagulls, and the small breathing holes left in the wet sand by clams and small crabs.

'Right. Now we cook the way they do in Hawaii,' said Vim. 'We have to dig a pit, line it with stones, build a fire, and cook our fish on the hot stones. It'll be the best fish you ever had.'

Vim went with Paul to collect dry branches and brush from the sandhills that rose in high steps above the bay. Jock and Kate started gathering water-washed pebbles and rocks near the tall jagged granite sentinels where the bay curved out into the sea. They were careful not to take all the stones from one place, and disturb the rock crabs and other creatures that lived there as little as possible. They filled a dive bag, and between them, each taking a handle, walked back to where the lunch box was.

'I'm going to start digging the pit now,' said Kate.

'Good idea,' said Jock.

Kate squatted on her heels. She began scooping out the sand, pushing it aside, fast and energetically.

'You look like old Towser, the dog we had when I used to live with my Mum and Dad,' said Jock.

'I don't look like an old dog at all!' said Kate indignantly. She dug even more furiously, making sand fly in all directions.

'Watch out!' said Jock. 'That went in my eyes.'

'You watch out,' said Kate.

'Let me do it – you're dangerous,' said Jock.

He came to kneel beside her. Kate had dug quite a sizeable hole.

'You've done enough,' Jock said.

Kate decided to take out just one more handful.

'Hold on,' said Jock. 'Stop.'

Kate stopped digging. But it wasn't because Jock told her to. She was looking in the hole. Jock looked too. They were both puzzled by what they saw. The bottom of the hole was no longer pure white. Kate leant in and scooped up a handful of sand from the bottom of the hole. She trickled it through her fingers. The sand, it was shiny! It glinted. And it was black!

Kate and Jock looked at one another, shocked. Jock was the first to speak.

'Ilmenite! In Dutchman's Bay.'

'What will that mean?' asked Kate, searching Jock's face.

Jock looked around him at the untouched beautiful wilderness of rocks, sand and sea.

'They can't mine here!' Kate said in a hushed voice, appalled.

'Let's cover it up and keep it a secret – pretend we don't know,' said Jock.

Kate hesitated, but only for a second. Then she started frantically pushing the sand back in the hole as fast as she could, with Jock heaping it in from the other side. They pushed and scraped, filling in the hole as fast as they could. But then a shadow fell over them. It was Paul and Vim with the firewood.

'What on earth are you doing?' said Vim.

Jock looked at Kate. What should they do? Could they keep it a secret? And from Vim? It hardly seemed possible.

But Kate's face had already crumpled.

'We've found ilmenite,' she said.

'What!' said Vim and Paul together, both horrified.

'It's true,' said Jock.

Vim scraped in the sand. He revealed the shiny black ilmenite. He jumped to his feet.

'Sorry about lunch,' he said. 'We'll have to go and see your Dad. We'll have to do something about getting this area protected.'

Together they ran to the rubber dinghy, carrying the unpacked lunch box.

'What will we do?' asked Paul as Vim rowed them back to the *Isabella*.

'I don't know,' said Vim, 'But we will have to think of something. We can't have sand mining here – not until we've proved whether the *Golden Falcon* is in the bay or not. They'll be blasting the reef for sure.' Vim's face was grim.

'Please hurry, Vim,' said Kate.

They all felt a desperate sense of urgency.

Meanwhile, Mrs Yates was resting under a shady tree watching Mr Scott and the Committee dig Brady out of the sand for a second time. They dug, they pushed, they sweated in the hot sun, until finally the truck was free. Brady, gruff and embarrassed, mumbled.

'Much obliged. Thanks a lot.' However, he couldn't resist saying to Mr Scott, 'I'll see you later, Bob, and we'll finalise those papers.' Then he got into his truck and very carefully drove off.

'Jack never gives up, does he?' said Frank, mopping sweat and dust from his face.

'An option is an option,' said Mr Scott. 'It's not a final contract.'

'Isn't it lunch time?' said Mrs Yates plaintively.

Frank had an idea. 'Why don't we leave going out to Dutchman's Bay until later?' he said. 'You could come to my place, Bob, and have a bit of lunch and a clean-up.'

'I'd appreciate that,' said Bob Scott.

'I think we could leave all this site examination to you gentlemen,' said Mrs Yates, unable to face more sandhills.

'You can manage without us, can't you?' said Miss Fitzgerald, who had a date to go swimming with the new young policeman that afternoon.

'Will you leave it to Alf and me?' said Frank.

'Suits me,' said Harry.

'Then that's fixed,' said Frank.

Alf, Frank and Mr Scott arrived back at the house at just about the same time that Vim and the kids were tying up the *Isabella* at the jetty. The settlement seemed deserted as they ran through the town, desperately anxious to get to Frank.

'Dad will think of something,' Paul assured Vim as they reached the Ellerys' front gate.

'Well, he's here anyway,' said Kate, indicating Alf and Frank's vehicles parked at the front.

They ran up the side path and burst into the kitchen.

'Dad . . .!' began Paul.

Then they all stopped. There was an unexpected guest – Mr Scott, who was now dabbing sunburn lotion on his burnt face.

'Oh,' said Paul.

'Hi, kids! G'day, Vim,' said Frank cheerfully. 'Just in time for lunch – the more the merrier.'

Paul hesitated, uncertain what to do. He looked at

Vim. None of them had counted on Mr Scott being with Frank. They couldn't say anything about ilmenite in front of him.

'I thought you'd still be diving,' said Alf. 'We were coming out to see you later.

'You were coming to see us?' said Vim, looking from Alf to Bob Scott. 'Why?' His tone was curt and suspicious.

Frank was a little surprised at the way Vim had spoken.

'Well – we've been talking it over and Bob here is considering taking up the sand lease at Dutchman's Bay instead of Jack Brady's land at Geelup Cove.' He said this with a smile, sure that this news would please Kate and Paul.

Vim, Kate and the boys could scarcely take this in. The sand mining company knew about the sand deposit already! No! Now there was no way of keeping it secret.

'But we didn't want anyone to know about that,' said Kate. 'We weren't going to tell anybody.' Her face filled with dismay.

'Well,' said Frank, 'it seems a good idea – it would be away from town.'

'We've always known about the sand at Dutchman's Bay,' said Mr Scott.

'But that's where the *Golden Falcon* is!' Paul burst out.

'Oh no! Not you too!' said Alf. 'Dorothy Yates has been talking about nothing else! People have been looking for that old wreck for fifty years to my knowledge and nothing's ever been found.'

'I've got new information,' said Vim.

'We have to think of the fact that Falcon Island needs permanent work for people,' said Frank. 'There's been nothing regular since the fish canning factory closed down six years ago. . . .'

Paul couldn't believe what he was hearing.

'. . . and if the mine was well away from the settlement, I think it would be a good thing.'

'You can't say that, Dad!' protested Paul.

'We have to face facts,' said Frank.

He looked at his son with understanding and sympathy. What Paul didn't realise was that, without jobs for the families, the island would cease to support even a small Council, and they would have to leave as others had. Tourists weren't enough to keep the island going. However, Frank knew that Paul would never accept that argument. His belief in the existence of the *Golden Falcon* was unshakeable.

'If sand mining takes place in Dutchman's Bay, the reef would have to be blasted, wouldn't it?' said Vim. 'So that the barges could get in.'

'Probably,' said Mr Scott.

Vim was looking grim.

'Have you any proof that the wreck is in Dutchman's Bay?'

'No actual proof,' said Vim. 'Just a conviction.'

The atmosphere was tense.

'If you could prove that the wreck was in Dutchman's Bay it would definitely be a factor my company would consider,' said Mr Scott. 'But in the absence of proof I feel that we are more likely to mine in Dutchman's Bay – it overcomes many of the local people's objections.' Bob Scott looked at Frank and Alf. They both nodded in agreement.

'It really will suit everyone better,' said Frank.

'Everyone except us!' said Jock bitterly.

'Look, kids. . . .' Frank began.

Vim spoke. 'How long have we got?'

'We won't be starting for about a month,' said Bob Scott.

'We'll get proof,' said Paul.

'Yes. We will!' said Kate and Jock.

The irony the situation now contained would have made Vim laugh if he hadn't been so upset.

'Have you told Jack Brady that you won't be taking up his land?' he asked.

Mr Scott suddenly looked battle-fatigued. 'That is a problem I have yet to face,' he said.

Kate and the boys went back to the jetty with Vim.

'We're not going to give up, are we?' asked Paul anxiously.

A shadowy look came into Vim's eyes. His passion was to be free. He didn't want involvement, argument and stress. But perhaps it was inevitable that life must contain these factors. He didn't answer at once. He thought deeply, as he had been doing for some weeks. The silence hung on, with Paul looking worriedly at Vim. But then the shadow passed from Vim's eyes.

'We'll find it! We've got to save it now – for those old Dutchmen!'

'Whoopee!' said Jock. It sounded almost like a war cry.

'We'll keep going until we find it!' said Paul.

Together Vim and the kids began to work out a more extensive exploration plan. They would dive every day, after school and weekends.

'We'll have to make every second count,' said Vim.

Within a few days Mr Scott rang Frank and made the news official. The company would mine in Dutchman's Bay.

In the town the information about the ilmenite deposit in Dutchman's Bay and the sand mining company's intention to mine there instead of at Geelup Cove was welcomed by most of the islanders who wanted peace. Everyone was fed up with the arguing that had been going on. And as Dutchman's Bay was so remote and difficult to reach, its existence didn't mean much to many people, so if there was to be mining, Dutchman's Bay seemed to be the answer.

But there were at least two people who disagreed violently. One was Mrs Yates, the other was Brady.

Frank and Alf found out what Brady's opinion was when they saw him near the Post Office on Wednesday afternoon.

Brady came hurtling towards them. He was practically incandescent with fury.

'What the hell have you two fools done?' he yelled.

'Hold on a minute, Jack,' said Alf. 'What's this about . . .?' But Alf's mild tone only seemed to increase Brady's rage.

'Don't take that line,' shouted Brady, 'as if you didn't know – you've done me out of my right and proper entitlements.'

'I'm sorry, Jack,' Frank began. And he genuinely did feel sorry. But Brady swept him aside.

'Something in it for you, is there?'

'What do you mean?' said Frank.

'Money. Money, of course – you get something out of it, don't you? You get a kick back I suppose. You could put your jobs on the line . . . Dutchman's Bay is Council land. . . .'

'Are you implying that Alf and I would get up to anything crooked?' said Frank coldly.

'Well, there's got to be some reason for Bob Scott changing his mind and not taking up my lease!'

Alf's face was set.

'If I hear you say a thing like that again, I won't be responsible for my actions,' said Alf. His tone was so cold, so threatening, that it was more effective than any bluster. Brady stepped back a bit.

'Well . . . naturally, I thought. . . .' he began.

'Then don't think like that,' said Alf. His eyes were as hard and coldly metallic as steel.

'Oh well,' said Brady, backing off further. He could see that he had overstepped the mark. He had memories of what Alf could be like when he got angry. They'd had a few run-ins in the past. Brady thought that he'd better be a bit conciliatory.

'Yeah . . . well, I suppose I got a bit heated.'

'Look, Jack,' said Frank, still feeling that Jack Brady was owed an explanation, 'the sand mining company makes its own decisions. . . .'

'What decisions?' demanded Mrs Yates at Frank's elbow.

'Dorothy!' said Frank. He hadn't seen her come.

'If you're talking about Dutchman's Bay, I can tell you my opinion. . . .' said Mrs Yates.

'Indeed,' said Alf, wondering if there would be more trouble.

'Yes!' she said. 'You needn't think I'm going to avoid my public responsibilities.'

'Oh, no!' said Frank.

'In fact I'm going to get up a petition to save our historic site. I'm going to rally all the islanders behind me.'

'That's only going to cause more problems, Dorothy,' said Frank.

'That might be your point of view,' said Mrs Yates. 'But I for one would never forgive myself if I didn't fight. I've started the petition today.'

Frank was about to remonstrate with Mrs Yates – the Committee, after all, supported the Dutchman's Bay site – but he was arrested by becoming aware of Brady and an unusually genial grin spreading over his face.

'I'll sign yer petition,' said Brady.

'Will you?' said Mrs Yates. 'You can do it straightaway if you like, Mr Brady.'

'Too right!' said Brady.

Frank and Alf stood in amazement watching Mrs Yates and Brady crossing the road together – the ample Mrs Yates like a fully rigged galleon and wiry Brady like a little shrimp boat.

Alf started to laugh.

'Mrs Yates and Brady – wonders will never cease!'

Frank chuckled too. It certainly was an unlikely

combination. But underneath he felt more than a bit bothered. The arguments about the mine being so close to the town would begin all over again. The fabric of the island community could be torn apart. From the bottom of his heart, Frank's most profound wish was that ilmenite had never been discovered on Falcon Island.

Chapter 11

The next week passed in a blur for Paul, Kate and Jock. They were out on the *Isabella* with Vim every moment they could spare. Vim was fishing only an hour or two every day, just enough to satisfy his deliveries to the fishing co-op. The rest of the time he was diving.

The area they had to search, the grottoes, caverns and tunnels in Dutchman's Bay, was so vast that at times their task seemed impossible – like trying to empty the bay with a spoon.

After the first week they weren't the only people in the bay. Mr Scott, surveyors and site planners were often tramping about on the dunes. However, the presence of men from the sand mining company only acted as a spur. Hour after hour they searched, becoming deeply tanned and their hair bleached – even Jock's dark brown hair was turning gold because of the constant exposure to sun and sea.

'We're going to do it. We're going to prove it,' Vim said as he checked his charts again. But despite his optimism they found nothing. And secretly they were beginning to wonder how long their search would take – would they find the *Golden Falcon* before the sand mining operations began? Time was against them.

During this period, Frank was far from happy. He and Paul had always been close, and now there seemed to be a gulf between them. It was obvious from the way Paul spoke and reacted that he felt that Frank had betrayed their closeness by supporting the move to mine in Dutchman's Bay. Frank was saddened by this, but he came to the conclusion that all he could do was to allow the kids to continue diving, even though they got tired and were neglecting other things, like homework and household jobs. He felt that Paul must be free to pursue the compulsion of his dream – the finding of the ancient Dutch wreck.

Mrs Yates was having difficulties as well. Each afternoon she shut the shop early and set off to tramp around the island getting signatures for her petition. She managed to persuade some of the doubters to sign but it was hard going. Brady got a few signatures as well.

After the best part of a week Mrs Yates could see that she wasn't going to get any further. However, she felt she had enough names to proceed to the next part of her plan. She arranged with Mrs Mortimer to look after her shop for a day, and took herself off to the city. She didn't tell anyone what she was doing, but she came back on the ferry with a very pleased look on her face. She still kept quiet about what she was up to.

It was Friday afternoon of the second week. In all that time, Vim, Paul and Jock, despite a thorough, meticulous search of the caverns, grottoes, reef and sea floor, had found nothing. They were even starting to go over areas they had already searched. Finally, Vim wearily gave the signal for them to go up.

Jock, on deck, pulled his wet suit off in despair. His usual cheerful face was downcast.

'We're getting nowhere,' he said. There was no doubt about it, they were all suffering from depression and a sense of failure.

'I wish I could help,' said Kate forlornly. She looked up to the sandhills. Already Dutchman's Bay was dotted with orange and red plastic markers indicating where a road should go and where the top layer of sand would be shifted to. The contour lines, marked with stakes, looked like rows of small fences – almost suburban. Dutchman's Bay had lost its aura of mystery. It was beginning to look like any other place on the coast because people had come. It made Kate feel very sad.

Vim and the boys had definitely almost reached the end of their endurance.

'I reckon we're beaten,' Jock repeated.

Vim lay back wearily against the rails of the deck. Tired lines showed around his eyes – his mind was going round and round, mentally checking all the details of his research, the information he had painstakingly gained. There was no doubt about it – everything that he had read indicated that Dutchman's Bay must be where the *Golden Falcon* had been wrecked. But it seemed that there must be some flaw in his calculations. For the hundredth time he went through the details of the last sighting of the *Golden Falcon*. Where could an error lie? Suddenly he sat bolt upright.

'My God—' he said.

'What?' said Paul, alerted by the tone of Vim's voice.

'There's something so obvious – I didn't think of it – I wonder.' He was already on his feet and heading for the cabin where his charts were laid out.

'What – what is it?' said Paul, Jock and Kate, crowding after him.

'Old measurements,' said Vim over his shoulder, as he frantically pulled down some old books and charts from the overhead locker.

'But what?' they demanded.

'Not sure,' said Vim. 'I'll have to work it out!'

Ever since Mrs Yates had paid her visit to the mainland, she had been anxiously waiting for the mail. Each day she had been disappointed until Friday afternoon of the second week, when a small mailbag arrived on the last ferry for the day.

Mrs Yates opened the bag. Then she saw what she was waiting for – a letter with a government seal. Two, in fact. One addressed to herself, the other to Mr Scott. Nervously she opened her letter. It was from the Minister for Lands, and very official. But as she read her face cleared – the information in it was better than she'd hoped for by far. The text was very brief but to the point. Summing up, it said, '. . . that under the provisions of the Museum Act, until the matter of the wreck in Dutchman's Bay was clarified, all permits to mine Dutchman's Bay would be deferred.'

'Ha, ha!' said Mrs Yates out aloud. 'Now we'll see what Mr Scott thinks of this!' With that she tidied herself up, put on a scarf and, taking Mr Scott's letter as well as her own, she shut the store, leaving a 'Delivering a telegram, back in ten minutes' sign on the door.

Finding Mr Scott didn't take long. She met Frank on the way and he gave her a lift to the small construction office that the mining company had set up in the camping area.

Mr Scott looked up with a smile when Mrs Yates and Frank arrived at his tent.

'What can I do for you?' he said.

'Personal delivery!' said Mrs Yates as she handed over the letter.

Mr Scott, surprised, took the letter. He opened it, reading quickly. Then he put it on the table. He was silent for a moment. Then with a gesture of resignation he said to Frank:

'Did you know about this?'

'Yes,' said Frank. He'd learned about it as they'd driven out. 'Dorothy has just told me.'

'This is not the best solution to our mutual problems, Mrs Yates,' said Mr Scott.

Mrs Yates was not deterred by Mr Scott's and Frank's attitudes.

'Somebody had to save the *Golden Falcon* – I was the only one prepared to act.

'If the *Golden Falcon* is in Dutchman's Bay,' said Frank.

'Why do you think the bay is called Dutchman's Bay?' said Mrs Yates sweepingly.

'I don't think that's a good enough reason to believe the wreck's there,' said Frank.

'Of course it is . . .' began Mrs Yates, ready for quite an argument, but Mr Scott butted in.

'Well, you've won, Mrs Yates,' he said. 'Mining will now take place in Geelup Cove.'

'Wonderful!' beamed Mrs Yates.

Frank sighed. 'I wish I could feel happy about it,' he said.

On the *Isabella* Vim had been searching furiously through all his research notebooks and papers. It seemed that he would never find what he was looking for. However at last, in a historical pamphlet, he found the clue he needed.

'Here it is!' he said.

'Tell us!' demanded Kate and the boys, jumping out of their skins with curiosity and excitement.

'This,' said Vim, his finger travelling along the page as he slowly translated. 'In the old days there was a difference in measurement – the seventeenth-century sea mile was slightly shorter than the present sea mile – it says so here – and that would mean. . . .' Vim was hastily scribbling on a pad near his charts, 'That would mean a difference of not two sea miles, but less, and that . . .' he had now got out his compass and was measuring distances on his chart, '. . . if we take Dirk's Rock as the last fixed point, the final measurements would be. . . .'

As he finished calculating, a look of total incredulousness crossed his face. He put the compass down.

'I don't believe it,' he said.

'I can't stand this,' said Kate. 'Tell us!'

'These calculations,' said Vim slowly, 'based on the old measurements, mean that the *Golden Falcon* must have been wrecked – in Geelup Cove!'

There was a stunned silence.

'Say that again,' said Paul. Vim quickly checked his figures.

'Yes – Geelup Cove.'

'I don't believe it,' said Paul.

'Wow!' whistled Jock.

'Where I found the florin,' said Paul slowly.

'Yes!' said Vim, wryly. 'That's right!' Without knowing it, all the time Paul had been close to the right place.

It was hard for Paul to take that in. He looked almost bewildered.

'I'm sorry, kids,' said Vim. 'All that diving for nothing!'

'Well, at least', said Kate, 'it won't matter that they mine sand here.' She indicated Dutchman's Bay with its festoons of plastic markers.

Suddenly Paul felt extremely happy. It was fantastic and marvellous. They would find the *Golden Falcon* now, and the final resting place of the brave and tragic sailors who had set sail from Holland centuries before.

'What are we waiting for – let's go and see what we can find!' said Jock with a huge grin.

'Right!' said Vim, as excited as the kids.

He started the engine of the *Isabella*. She seemed to leap into life as if she understood their urgency, and to fly across the water, covering the distance from one side of the island to the other faster than she had ever done before. In no time they were coming into Geelup Cove. This time Vim anchored outside the reef and not within its shelter. He had checked and re-checked his calculations – everything indicated that the outside reef was the place to begin.

Within minutes, Vim and the boys were zipped into their wet suits. Kate, looking at Paul, could see that he was quite pale – his tension was obvious. And Paul was thinking – would they succeed? His heart was beating so hard it was almost like his first dive.

With a splash Vim went in, followed by Jock, then Paul. Vim signalled for Jock and Paul to follow. They swam for a short distance along the reef, which at this point was just a wall of coral, but ahead they could see where it projected out into a shelf, with tunnels that formed a labyrinth. As they swam they were tugged by the surge. Paul was glad the swell wasn't very big – he didn't like the thought of being slammed against the sharp coral wall by a running sea. It would bash them to bits.

When they reached the tunnel Vim checked it, then he indicated that they were to follow. They had to grope side by side along the tunnel, with the swell pushing them about, but eventually they made their way into a place where the tunnel opened into a chamber, partly enclosed by the overhead shelf, but with enough light from above to see clearly. The chamber was like the court of a medieval castle. There were other tunnels arched like old doorways all around, each one full of mystery.

Nobody knew who saw it first. Later they would talk about it endlessly, but now, five metres away, lying flukes up as if waiting for them, weed-covered and encrusted, wedged deeply between sections of the reef, was the unmistakable shape of an old, old anchor!

They swam fast towards it, their fins beating together in a tattoo of triumph. When they got to it, Vim quickly got out his knife and scraped away some weed. They knew what they were looking for – fine layers of metal that would indicate that the anchor had been riveted together, layer by layer, in a charcoal forge three hundred and fifty years before. And that was what they found. The anchor was undoubtedly Dutch in origin.

Back on deck, Vim was so excited that all he could do was to dance about in a jig of victory.

'We've done it! We've done it!' he said.

'I want to tell everyone,' said Kate, hugging him.

'I want to tell Nan and Pop,' said Jock.

'And I'm going to tell Dad,' said Paul with pride.

Nothing could have prepared Paul, Kate, Jock and Vim for the incredible numbing reaction that followed their jubilant, triumphant run from the jetty into the town square. They almost expected the church bells to ring and sirens to sound.

All Frank could say was, 'I'm sorry, kids – Vim – you're too late. Mining has been deferred in Dutchman's Bay by the Government. The company is going to mine Geelup Cove.'

'But don't you understand, Dad,' said Paul, desperately. 'The anchor's in Geelup Cove! It's where I found the florin – don't you understand!'

Frank looked at their despairing faces, he understood exactly how they felt, but there was nothing he could do. He shook his head.

'Sorry,' he said, 'but that's the way it is.'

'We were wrong about Dutchman's Bay – we can explain. . . .' Paul went on.

Vim interrupted. 'Where's Mr Scott?' he said. 'We'll talk to him.'

When they got to Mr Scott he at first thought they were playing some kind of joke.

'You islanders have got a peculiar sense of humour,' he said.

It took a few minutes to get him to understand that they were sure there was an old Dutch anchor in Geelup Cove.

Mr Scott, mild as his temperament was, was in danger of losing his temper. He began to count to ten. The way this project was going he'd be on the mat in Head Office any minute. He would have to answer for all this messing around. But, on the other hand, he had to consider – if by some chance they were proved to be right, and it wasn't just an old rusted fishing boat anchor, it was a factor he would have to take into account. His company didn't care for trouble with the authorities, especially the Maritime Museum.

So he said to Vim, 'Can you prove this? Can you lift this anchor?'

'No,' said Vim. 'It's firmly wedged into the reef.'

'Well,' said Mr Scott, 'there's nothing I can do about it – I have to have proof.'

'But it *is* there!' Kate protested with vehemence.

'Sorry – I need some sort of proof,' said Mr Scott. Then he added, 'I start in Geelup Cove on Monday week.'

'On Monday week?' echoed Paul.

'That's right,' said Mr Scott with finality.

In absolute dejection they wandered back to the jetty so that the kids could collect their gear. As they walked along the jetty they saw that Mrs Yates had come down with a basket of bread to feed the seagulls. At first it looked as if she wanted to avoid them. They could see that she was very upset. But after a minute or two she came back towards them.

'I've heard. I'm very sorry,' she said.

'Things travel fast in this place,' said Jock.

'What can I say?' said Mrs Yates. 'I was sure I was acting for the best.' Her distress was obvious.

'You meant well, Mrs Yates,' said Kate.

'You weren't to know,' said Paul.

'We didn't ourselves,' said Jock.

It was just about too much for Mrs Yates.

'What make me so angry,' said Vim, 'is that Mr Scott isn't prepared to take our word.'

'Well,' said Mrs Yates, 'I suppose . . . he's already tried to do the right thing . . . he has been quite patient. . . .'

'Maybe,' said Paul. 'But the important thing is to listen to us now, and he won't.'

'O.K. – Mr Scott won't listen to us,' said Jock. 'So what do we do?'

Mrs Yates looked helpless, and Vim hesitated, but there was no hesitation in Paul's mind. His determination was absolute.

'We've got a week – we'll find something. We'll get the proof!' he said.

It became a frantic race against time. Every moment they could snatch they dived on the shelf at Geelup Cove. They combed the area around the old anchor. They were scratched, torn and buffeted against the sharp rocks of the narrow tunnels under the shelf. To illuminate the dark holes and crevices, Vim acquired an underwater light. They dived before school and after school. They hacked and prised at the reef until their hands were bleeding, hoping to find something embedded in the coral. But it was all to no avail. They couldn't find anything. The boys were getting dark circles under their eyes despite their deep tan.

Then when they surfaced one afternoon they saw Brady on the reef. He had a plumb line and was sounding the reef.

'What's he doing?' asked Jock.

'By the look of it he's checking the depth,' said Vim.

'Why?' demanded Paul.

'I think he's working out where to blast to open the channel,' said Vim.

'But he can't,' said the kids.

'He will!' said Vim, grimly.

The whole desperate attempt suddenly seemed impossible. They were going to be beaten. And nobody except Mrs Yates, Nan, Alf and Frank – who were worrying about them all the time – seemed to care.

And then it was Sunday afternoon. It was only hours before Mr Scott would move his equipment out to Geelup Cove. The big machines, which had already arrived, would tear at the sandhills. The reef would be blasted, the Cove dredged. Never again would they be able to come to this gentle, peaceful place. It was going to be changed forever. And worse, any chance of saving the invaluable history of the island was almost over. It would be blown up when the charges of dynamite opened the channel.

By five o'clock on Sunday, they had been diving for hours. They were very, very tired, and there was a swell that was causing turbulence on the reef. They were constantly in danger of being dashed against the sharp surfaces of the rock, and now there was a growing likelihood that they could be caught in the underwater tunnels – the tide could suck them in, trapping them. And it was also becoming hard to see – the surge was causing the sand to swirl up, reducing visibility.

Wearily, Vim was ready to admit defeat. It was pointless. This site was so rough, so difficult that the sea had obviously destroyed all evidence of the wreck except the gallant anchor. He was about to give the signal to go up when suddenly Paul darted past him towards a patch of sand which was being disturbed by the onrush of the turning tide. Paul was scrabbling frantically – his hands were shaking so much he could hardly push the sand aside. Then Vim and Jock saw what Paul had seen – a glint, merely a glint, but silver! Silver!

Vim dashed towards Paul. His excitement was so intense he could scarcely get his knife from his belt. Jock was beside him. Vim hacked and gouged at the black mass on the sea floor. He struggled with it, but he couldn't get it free. Surely he wasn't going to be defeated now?

Jock was helping him, and Paul. They both had their knives, and Jock a small hammer. Jock used his knife as a wedge – then hit the material hard with his hammer. And then the lump of concretion with the glint of silver, broke free. Jock moved back. He signalled to a hesitant Paul, 'Pick it up!'

In wonder Paul picked it up. Through his mask he could see – there was no doubt – a fine thread of silver. Holding it carefully, Paul swam to the surface with Vim and Jock. All three had a great sense of victory that made all their effort and exhaustion seem worthwhile.

Within minutes of surfacing Vim had the concreted mass in a solution tank.

'Well, it's silver,' he said. 'But it's so concreted, it's hard to say what it is.'

'It's guilders for sure!' said Kate excitedly.

'Well – maybe,' said Vim. 'But it could be almost anything – buttons, a tankard, anything.'

'When will you know?' asked Paul anxiously.

'Twenty-four hours,' said Vim.

'But they start tomorrow morning,' said Jock.

'We'll tell them – and they won't start,' said Paul, sure of their victory.

But Paul was too confident too soon. The next morning the huge machines lumbered through the town square, ready to begin work on the site preparation for the opencast sand mine. There were bulldozers, scoops, trucks and front end loaders, led by Mr Scott with his foreman in a Land Rover.

On the side of the road, the kids flagged him down. Mr Scott was surprised. Nevertheless, he told his foreman to pull over to the side.

'Well,' he said, leaning out of the Land Rover, 'what can I do for you?'

'We've got proof, Mr Scott,' said Paul with proud confidence, his face alight. 'We've definitely got proof!'

'Have you?' said Mr Scott with a sigh. 'All right – let's see it.'

'Well, Vim's still working on it,' said Paul.

'What!' said Mr Scott, now really angry. 'What are you playing at? Go on – off you go!'

'But it's true!' said Kate.

'You're wasting my time. I've got work to do and this machinery costs money.'

'But. . . .'

'No!'

Mr Scott signalled to his foreman to drive on. He leant out of the window. 'When you're older you might find the old wreck,' he said.

The kids were left standing on the side of the road.

'We're beaten,' said Kate, shattered.

Paul was thinking rapidly.

'No we're not,' he said. 'Jock, you go and get Vim. Tell him to bring the silver. Go as fast as you can. Kate and I will stop them.'

'How?' said Jock.

'I'll think of something,' said Paul.

Jock wasn't sure, but he got on his bike and raced off. Paul didn't really know what he was going to do.

'What are we going to do, Paulie?' said Kate, nearly in tears.

'I don't know – we've got to think of something!'

Suddenly Kate's face cleared. Her blue eyes started to twinkle. Her face broke into a grin.

'I know!' she said.

'What?'

'The rest of the kids – from school.'

Paul took a second or two to understand what she meant. Then he realised.

'Brilliant – absolutely brilliant, Katey!' he said.

'Quick, come on!' They got on their bikes and dashed down the road.

At the school Kate and Paul rounded up everyone from Grade One to Grade Seven – the whole lot. Everyone was needed.

Mr Scott's convoy, now being led by Jack Brady in his truck, with his horn blowing in a trumpeting of victory, rounded the bend near the she-oak grove. As usual, the beautiful shadows fell across the road, and birds flitted from tree to tree. But then, without warning, the shadows of the she-oak grove seemed to part and out spilled a great mass of kids on bikes. The entire school. They spread across the road – a human barrier.

Brady swore and braked hard. Behind him, all the vehicles jolted to a stop, bumping and thumping into each other.

Mr Scott was out of his truck in a second.

'What the hell. . . .'

'Yeah . . . what the hell is this?' demanded Brady.

Mr Scott was furious.

'You children are blocking the road. Move off!'

'No,' said Paul.

'No,' said the rest of the school in a chorus.

'You can't do this,' said Scott.

'But we are,' said Paul.

'Get rid of these damn kids,' demanded Brady, puce with rage.

The drivers of the machines started to congregate, doors slamming.

'What's going on?' they demanded.

'We just want a bit of time,' said Paul. 'And then we can give you the proof, Mr Scott.'

'No!' shouted Brady.

But Mr Scott was stroking his chin reflectively. If these kids were so convinced that the *Golden Falcon* was in Geelup Cove, maybe they should have a chance to prove it.

'Please, Mr Scott,' said Kate.

'Please,' said all the other kids.

Who knows what did the trick? Kate's blue eyes, the integrity in Paul's face, the weight of numbers, or a sense of fair play.

'Half an hour then,' said Mr Scott.

'Tell them to clear off, you mean,' yelled Brady.

'An hour,' bargained Paul.

'Three-quarters,' said Mr Scott.

'Right!' said Paul, now very confident.

'O.K., men,' said Mr Scott. 'Tea break!'

Jock had got to the jetty in the fastest time ever.

'Paul says to come and bring the silver,' he said.

'But I can't shift the concretion,' said Vim, who had been working on the concreted mass since early daylight.

'Can't you do something?' said Jock.

'I'll try again,' said Vim, taking up a small pick and hammer. His brow furrowed in concentration, he tried again to clear away some of the concretion to reveal more than just the tantalising glimpse of silver.

Miss Fitzgerald had finished putting up the morning's work on the blackboard. She went to the verandah to ring the school bell. It was only then she realised how quiet everything was. There were no children. The school yard was empty, deserted.

Worried, she ran to the gate. No children. Then she ran down the road. She couldn't see any children anywhere.

Anxiety was starting to grow in the kids blocking the convoy. Paul in particular was now feeling worried. He had set the road block up. He was responsible. It mustn't fail. Please come, Vim, Paul was praying. Where are you? But the minutes ticked on. Mr Scott was calmly leaning against the Land Rover. He looked at his watch.

'Seventeen minutes, kids,' he said.

'Make them go now,' demanded Brady, as he had repeatedly.

Mr Scott ignored him.

'Fifteen minutes,' said Mr Scott.

Vim had now turned the concreted lump over. He still couldn't make an impression on it.

'Hurry, Vim,' urged Jock.

Vim took up a bigger mallet.

In the town a dishevelled Miss Fitzgerald rushed up to Frank and Alf.

'All the kids are missing!' she cried.

Vim was sweating. If he hit the concretion too hard he could shatter it, and the silver too, into fragments. He inserted a small chisel. He shut his eyes. He couldn't bear to hit it.

'Do it, Vim,' said Jock pleadingly.

Vim opened his eyes. He took aim and hit the concreted lump. It split wide open. Inside, nestling, perfect, was a round silver coin – several coins.

'What are they?' breathed Jock.

Vim picked up a magnifying glass.

'Guilders,' he said.

On the road the bunch of kids was getting restless. Paul's mouth was dry. He was trying not to panic. Brady had now taken it upon himself to announce the passing minutes.

'Five minutes,' said Brady.

Kate and Paul felt that they were measuring every second with their heartbeats.

'Four minutes,' said Brady.

Then a great phalanx of adults turned up – Miss Fitzgerald and Frank, Alf, Harry, Mrs Yates, Mrs Mortimer, Mr Meredith and others.

'What are you children doing?' demanded Miss Fitzgerald.

'Yes – what's going on?' said Alf.

'Kid power,' said Kate.

'Oh!' said Miss Fitzgerald.

'Break it up, kids,' said Frank.

'No,' said Paul desperately.

'Three minutes,' said Brady.

Mr Scott was beginning to feel sorry for Paul. He was obviously under stress and beginning to lose confidence. The men were starting to go back to their machines.

'One and a half,' counted Brady.

It was almost as if a countdown was going to explode and destroy them all.

'One,' said Brady. But his voice was drowned out.

There was a louder sound – a great shout. Everyone turned. It was Vim and Jock, running down the road. Their arms were over their heads like Olympic winners.

'Guilders . . . guilders!' shouted Vim.

'Guilders,' shouted Jock.

'Guilders!' breathed Paul in relief.

The reaction swept through the crowd, as Kate was running up the road to meet Vim.

'Those old Dutchmen didn't let you down, Vim!'

'Dutch guilders,' said Miss Fitzgerald with a happy smile.

Mrs Yates was kissing everyone. Frank shook Mr Scott's hand, Alf was congratulating Paul. Mr Meredith explained to the workmen what it was all about.

'Falcon Island has revealed its heritage,' he said.

Vim came striding down the white dusty road, Kate on his shoulders.

'We've won!' he said.

A great cheer went up from the crowd.

'Good work, Paul,' Frank said quietly. Paul grinned.

Brady had almost the last word.

'You're mugs, all of you,' said Brady, furiously, 'giving in to kids.'

'Sorry about that, Mr Brady,' said Jock.

But his wide smile belied his words.

More Beaver Books

We hope you have enjoyed this Beaver Book. Here are some of the other titles:

Echoes of Louisa A Beaver original. Allie, on holiday near historic Thornaby Hall, becomes part of a real-life drama that happened a hundred years before in this exciting and unusual ghost story for older readers by Gail Renard, which is based on the ATV production of the same name

Horse on a Hilltop Lolly is afraid of an old man whose cottage she has to pass to get to her pony's field – yet she *has* to exercise him every day so he will do well in the local show. An unusual pony story for readers of eight and over by Joanne Webster; illustrated by Trevor Parkin

250 More Things to Send Off For A Beaver original. Posters, wall-charts, jigsaws, jewellery, models to make – details of all kinds of exciting things you can send for through the post, most of which are either free or at pocket-money prices. Written by Elizabeth Gundrey, author of *Send Off For It*, and illustrated by Susie Lacome

These and many other Beavers are available from your local bookshop or newsagent, or can be ordered direct from: Hamlyn Paperback Cash Sales, PO Box 11, Falmouth, Cornwall TR10 9EN. Send a cheque or postal order made payable to the Hamlyn Publishing Group, for the price of the book plus postage at the following rates:
UK: 40p for the first book, 18p for the second book, and 13p for each additional book ordered to a maximum charge of £1.49;
BFPO and Eire: 40p for the first book, 18p for the second book, plus 13p per copy for the next 7 books and thereafter 7p per book;
OVERSEAS: 60p for the first book and 18p for each extra book.

New Beavers are published every month and if you would like the *Beaver Bulletin*, a newsletter which tells you about new books and gives a complete list of titles and prices, send a large stamped addressed envelope to:

Beaver Bulletin
Hamlyn Paperbacks
Banda House
Cambridge Grove
London W6 0LE

20555X